SEVEN DEADLY LAWSUITS

Seven Deadly Lawsuits

HOW MINISTERS CAN AVOID LITIGATION AND REGULATION

Thomas F. Taylor

ABINGDON PRESS
NASHVILLE

SEVEN DEADLY LAWSUITS:
HOW MINISTERS CAN AVOID LITIGATION AND REGULATION

This book is printed on recycled, acid-free paper.

Library of Congress Cataloging-in-Publication Data

Taylor, Thomas F., 1959-
  Seven deadly lawsuits : how ministers can avoid litigation and regulation / Thomas F. Taylor.
    p. cm.
  Includes bibliographical references.
  ISBN 0-687-00822-0 (pbk. : alk. paper)
    1. Clergy—Legal status, laws, etc.—United States. 2. Actions and defenses—Unites States.   I. Title.
  KF4868.C44T39   1996
  174'.1—dc20   96-455
                                                             CIP

96 97 97 99 00 01 02 03 04 05—10 9 8 7 6 5 4 3 2 1

MANUFACTURED IN THHE UNITED STATES OF AMERICA

To Dad and Mom,
the Reverend Thomas F. Taylor and Phyllis J. Taylor,
for your lives of ministry,
integrity, and compassion toward
so many

CONTENTS

ACKNOWLEDGMENTS

I thank the many who have contributed to the writing of this book through research, editing, and practical suggestions. I especially thank the following attorneys for their contributions: W. Brian Hulse, Jeff T. Sivertsen, and Mark O. Morris, of the Salt Lake City office of Snell & Wilmer. I thank Greg Nielson, the managing attorney of that office, for his gracious invitation to use their library and research facilities. I owe a debt of gratitude to attorney Kim R. Wilson of Snow, Christensen & Martineau in Salt Lake City, for his tireless review of the entire manuscript, and to attorney Jack Morgan of Kimball, Parr, Waddoups, Brown, and Gee in Salt Lake City, for his detailed research of child-abuse reporting laws. I thank attorney David Watkiss of Watkiss, Dunning & Watkiss in Salt Lake City for his expertise in reviewing the chapter on defamation. I am grateful to Robert Stutz of Hopkins and Sutter in Chicago for reviewing the introduction and other chapters, and to Salt Lake attorneys Steve Aeschbacher, Steve Hill, and Assitant Attorney General of Utah, Craig Barlow, for their review of and suggestions for the sexual-misconduct chapter.

I thank my wife, Jan, for acting as a sounding board for numerous portions of the book, even during our first year of marriage and our first pregnancy.

I thank the Abingdon staff for their enormously helpful suggestions and edits in the final stages of this book.

ACKNOWLEDGMENTS

Finally, I may owe my greatest thanks to legal secretary Marcia Deckart, of the law offices of Snell & Wilmer, for her painstaking transcription of much of the manuscript, which saved countless hours at the computer keyboard.

PREFACE

I have worked full-time both as an attorney and as a minister. To my surprise, in many ways I received more respect as an attorney. In the law, I was frequently asked lofty philosophical questions like, "How do you ethically defend someone you know is guilty?" In ministry, I am often asked things such as, "What do you do all week, anyway?" When people learned that I was a full-time attorney, they often chided me with a mediocre lawyer joke—at which they heartily laughed. Thereafter, however, they often deferentially and earnestly asked legal advice about a car accident they were involved in, or the legal liability of a neighbor whose dog bit their child. When I tell people I am a minister, too often they feign an unconvincing seriousness, then say something noncommittal like, "Oh . . . interesting." In the law, I was paid extremely well. In ministry, I am paid enough.

We live in a post-Christian age, even a postmodern age. Most people no longer observe life from the standpoint of a Christian, or even a religious worldview. They know increasingly less about ministry and ministers. The result is that society has lost a once-held social reverence for ministers. For better or worse, society prides itself in treating clergy and all other professionals with the same disinterest and detachment—especially in our courts of law. Our job as ministers is to prepare to adjust to this new society. This book is a tool for that preparation.

PREFACE

This is not a book about all lawsuits against ministers, or even the most frequently brought actions. It is a book about the most damaging kinds of lawsuits against ministers—damaging to their finances, emotions, and reputations.

Although this book may aid attorneys in learning about some of the seminal cases in church law, it was not written specifically for them. Instead, it is written for those preparing for, and presently engaged in, all kinds of ministry. The intent here is not to offer legal advice for any specific legal problem. Readers with a legal problem should seek an attorney licensed to practice law in their state for such advice.

I offer this book, however, with the hope and prayer that it will instruct ministers about laws that may affect them, that it will prepare pastors, workers with children and youth, seminary professors and students, chaplains, counselors, Christian camp workers, and all others who are involved in any kind of ministry, to carry out their work in the coming century with dignity, integrity, and honor. May this work raise the level of ministers' consciences to "live lives worthy of the calling they have received."

THOMAS F. TAYLOR

This author is available as a speaker for churches, pastors' conferences, retreats, colleges, and seminaries, on issues regarding Christianity, the law, and ethics. For bookings, contact:

First Presbyterian Church
12 "C" Street
Salt Lake City, Utah 84103
Telephone: 801-363-3889
Fax: 801-363-1344

Consider Yourself Served

Not many of you should become teachers, my brothers and sisters, for you know that we who teach will be judged with greater strictness.

JAMES 3:1

Upon finishing what he considered one of his better sermons at the close of the Sunday morning service, the Reverend Steve Barnett saw a man heading down the aisle toward him. The stranger smiled as he approached. Steve, delighted, prepared to greet the new visitor.

The man extended his hand, saying, "Reverend Barnett?"

Steve answered, "Yes. And what's your name? I don't believe I've met you."

"Consider yourself served," the man said, handing Steve some stapled papers.

Steve took the papers, and the man turned and walked back down the aisle and out the church doors. The document looked official. The first page read "Complaint" in bold print.

After momentary confusion, Steve realized that he had just been served with a lawsuit. He thought, "There must be some mistake." He could recall nothing that he had done that would invite a lawsuit. But there was no mistake. What could he do? What would his parishioners say? How much would all this cost? And how would he respond to, or even understand the complicated legal claims brought against him?

This book is about lawsuits against pastors, religious workers, churches, and religious organizations.[1] It is especially concerned with lawsuits that make moral as well as legal claims against the clergy. Scenes such as the one described have become more common than many of us might like to think. The ensuing lawsuit may cause irreparable damage to a lifetime of ministry or to a church.

During the last two decades, the American legal system has undergone startling developments that will affect all clergy, religious workers, and churches—regardless of denomination or religion. For events occurring in the church counseling office and in the church board room, the American public is suing its religious leaders and organizations at an unprecedented rate. Complaining parties and their attorneys are asserting new causes of action, such as clergy malpractice and breach of confidentiality. Churches are being held legally responsible for the acts or omissions of their employees.

Whether Americans choose to view these dramatic changes on the legal landscape as a threat to religious liberty, or as the mere imposition of reasonable restrictions on an otherwise favored aspect of American life, lawsuits that affect religious workers are a reality and are costly. Even when lawsuits are unsuccessful, the recipients of the summonses and complaints often experience the trauma and stress of years of litigation, as well as the often devastating financial losses incurred in attorneys' fees while defending the suits.

Although religious workers and organizations enjoy certain freedoms under the First Amendment to the United States Constitution, courts and legislatures have made it increasingly clear that even ministers may be held accountable when their acts are suffiently injurious to the interests of others.

This book, however, is not about how to "fight back" against such claims. That is a matter best left to the lawyer handling an individual case, after the alleged damage has been done. Instead, this book advises clergy, religious workers, and organizations how to educate themselves about the kinds of lawsuits that could be levied against them in years to come and practical ways they can avoid costly legal involvement in the first place.

Before examining the specific kinds of lawsuits that have been levied against clergy, the remainder of this section will consider the difference between lawsuits that allege both legal and moral wrongdoing, and suits that typically are thought of as merely legal. Next we'll be given a snapshot of where ministers and churches stand in the American legal system, as indicated by the receptivity of courts to lawsuits brought against them. Finally, several fundamental aspects of the American legal system important for understanding the rest of the book will be explained.

MORALITY AND THE LAW

It may seem obvious that suing a minister for moral wrongdoing often is worse than asserting a strictly legal violation. But these distinctions are more subtle than they first appear.

Despite the often touted claim, "you can't legislate morality," the reality is that we, as Americans, legislate morality daily. It is true that under the United States Constitution, we cannot enact a law with the primary purpose or effect of advancing a religious viewpoint. However, American law is replete with rules and prohibitions considered by most to have a moral base. Adultery statutes still exist in most states. Laws against murder, theft, and committing intentional personal injury exist in some form in every state. That such laws are found also in the Bible and other ancient religious literature should not surprise us. Many of our modern laws have their origins in ancient traditions and communities, where the distinctions between law, morality, and religion were not clearly drawn. Obviously then, many of our laws still have moral as well as legal underpinnings and implications.

Conversely, some of our laws seem remedial and practical in nature. We might call them purely legal.[2] They are helpful in arranging and ordering society, and their purpose is to serve the daily functions carried out by society. But they do not appear particularly moral.[3] Not stopping completely at a stop sign on a lonely country road at 3:00 A.M. may be illegal, but such an act would not strike most of us as immoral. Many of us have driven over the speed limit at one time or another, but we would not expect to be accused of having poor character, based on that violation alone.

Seven Deadly Sins—Seven Deadly Lawsuits

What are the implications, from society's standpoint, for ministers and religious workers of all kinds, that some laws appear to be more morally based than others? This question may best be answered by a brief historical overview of the origins of moral and legal development in the western world.

The Bible

Most ministers are (or should be) fully aware that society has long despised some bad acts more than others. Historically, the practice of distinguishing certain bad acts as egregious and meting out heavier penalties for those acts, has religious roots. Although somewhat oversimplified, a brief sketch reveals that these roots stretch back to biblical times.[4]

Since the earliest days of the Old and New Testament communities, religious leaders have exhorted believers to live lives of holiness, avoiding sin. The reasons given were that sin is antithetical to and alienates us from God, who is holy (Isa. 59:2; Ps. 51:1-12; Luke 5:8), and that sin has destructive earthly consequences (Isa. 59:2-7; Rom. 3:23; 5:12). In the Old Testament, we read such early exhortations:

> "You have seen what I did to the Egyptians, and how I bore you on eagles' wings and brought you to myself. Now therefore, if you obey my voice and keep my covenant, you shall be my treasured possession out of all the peoples. Indeed, the whole earth is mine, but you shall be for me a priestly kingdom and a holy nation. These are the words that you shall speak to the Isrelites."
>
> So Moses came, summoned the elders of the people, and set before them all these words that the LORD had commanded him. The people all answered as one: "Everything that the LORD has spoken we will do." Moses reported the words of the people to the LORD.
>
> Exodus 19:4-8

Similarly, in the New Testament, the earliest exhortations by church leaders instructed the community of believers not to sin:

> See that none of you repays evil for evil, but always seek to do good to one another and to all. . . . but test everything; hold fast to what is good; abstain from every form of evil.
>
> I Thessalonians 5:15, 21-22

Both Jewish and Christian communities also quickly realized, however, that believers were unwilling or unable to stop sinning altogether (see e.g., Exod. 32:7-8; I Cor. 5:1). It was also clear that some people sinned more often or more severely than others. These realities required religious leaders to teach the believing communities means of atonement (Exod. 32:30; I Cor.

5:5). Elaborate atonement sacrifices were instituted in the Old Testament Jewish community (Lev. 1–7,16) involving confession of the sin (Lev. 5:5). In the New Testament Christian community, while many of the same Old Testament sacrifices were not retained (Acts 15:19-20), confession of sins was promoted as the means of reestablishing relations with God (I John 1:9).

An even more elaborate sociotheological development occurred in the recognition that some sins were of greater social consequence than others. Killing your neighbor's goat had far less social import than killing your neighbor. Laws were established in the Pentateuch and other Old Testament writings to distinguish some sins as worse then others, by attaching more severe punishments or remedies to certain acts. For instance, the penalty for violating food laws was expulsion from the Israelite community (Lev. 7:24-25), whereas the penalty for committing adultery was death (Lev. 20:10). Likewise, leaders in the earliest Christian church acknowledged that some sins merited greater retribution. Jesus recognized as unforgivable the sin against the Holy Spirit (Matt. 12:31-32; Mark 3:28-30; Luke 12:10). Paul taught that participation in certain sins excluded one from the kingdom of God (I Cor. 6:9; Gal. 5:21). John recognized a clear distinction in the serious consequences of some sins over others:

> If you see your brother or sister committing what is not a mortal sin, you will ask, and God will give life to such a one—to those whose sin is not mortal. There is sin that is mortal; I do not say that you should pray about that. All wrongdoing is sin, but there is sin that is not mortal.
>
> I John 5:16-17 (see also Heb. 6:4-6)

These texts and acts of the ancient Jewish and Christian communities represent early legislative efforts to make a given punishment fit the crime (or wrongdoing)—an equitable maxim also recognized in our western legal heritage.

Along with the teaching that some acts were "worse" than others came the presumption that religious leaders themselves were to be held to higher standards of behavior than the laity. This was only logical, since the laity looked to religious teachers for spiritual leadership (Mark 7:5-6; Luke 17:1; Rom. 2:21-23; I Tim. 3:1-15). The book of James states this most pointedly:

Not many of you should become teachers, my brothers and sisters, for you know that we who teach will be judged with greater strictness.

James 3:1

Church History

By the second and third centuries, the church Fathers had further developed the doctrines espoused in the New Testament, especially those holding that some sins were worse than others, or at least had more negative social consequences than others.

In his work *On Modesty,* Tertullian describes sins as falling into one of two categories: (1) pardonable sins, resulting in chastisement; and (2) irremissible penalties, resulting in condemnation.[5] By the Middle Ages, the Roman Catholic Church had at least two categories for sins. Lesser sins, usually those that were not truly voluntary and for which forgiveness was possible, were called *venial* sins. Sins that affected one's salvation (i.e., one's eternal standing with God) became known as *deadly* or *mortal* sins.

Not everyone in the church agreed on which sins were venial and which were spiritually deadly. But by the time of Pope Gregory I (c. 540–604), a list of seven sins was formally recognized as those that were "deadly."[6] Gregory's list of seven sins included pride, covetousness or greed, lust, envy, gluttony, anger, and sloth or laziness.[7] Thomas Aquinas cited Gregory's list in a discussion of the seven "capital sins" in his *Summa Theologiae* 1-2.84.4. In 1689, Saint Ignatius of Loyola discussed the same list of seven deadly sins in his *Spiritual Exercises.*

The list of seven deadly sins may seem remarkably tame by today's standards. Nevertheless, Loyola and his predecessors who wrote about them considered them quintessentially bad, and thus labeled them "deadly." By Loyola's time, a few things were surely clear to the laity regarding behavior. First, no one wanted to be accused of any of the seven deadly sins, not only because they were associated with spiritual death, but also because they evoked social disdain. Second, the church and its leaders established themselves as the custodians and spokespeople for morality and moral issues. Finally, because church leaders taught that certain of these sins were especially bad, most people logically assumed that the relgious leaders, in particular, would avoid willfully engaging in the worst of these acts.

Ancient Law/Modern Law

Like their ancient counterparts, modern societies punish people for their bad acts more severely, and often attach moral disdain to them, when the wrongdoing is done willfully or intentionally, or when they violate the customarily accepted rights or duties of the community. Such acts often are referred to by modern courts as acts of moral turpitude.[8] Although few such bad acts merit the death penalty now as in ancient times, they often carry with them penalties greater than do the bad acts with no moral implications.

Modern laws governing moral conduct tend to be more detailed than were the laws of many ancient societies. Modern laws, whether statutory or from judicial precedent, keenly look out for the welfare of individuals or groups that cannot otherwise look out for themselves, such as children, the mentally impaired, the elderly, or others who may be vulnerable in many circumstances.

Today's laws also recognize and sometimes regulate certain kinds of relationships considered special in some way or another by legislatures and courts. These often are known as fiduciary relationships. *Fiduciary* comes from a Latin term meaning "trust." A fiduciary relationship may be created when one party entrusts his well-being to another for a specific purpose. Such a relationship is likely to be created if one of the parties has an upper hand in some way, either because one knows something the other does not, or is stronger than the other in some relevant respect.

Counseling relationships often are considered by courts to be fiduciary relationships, especially when one party is an adult and the other a minor, when the counselee is elderly or so depressed that he or she is unable to think clearly, or is highly susceptible to the influence of the counselor. An individual who is a fiduciary to another owes a higher than ordinary degree of care and loyalty to that person. Supreme Court Justice Benjamin Cardozo once stated that a fiduciary "is held to something stricter than the morals of the marketplace."[9] As later chapters will reveal, some courts may view certain relationships between ministers and parishioners as fiduciary relationships.

Thus, while modern laws are usually more complex and less explicitly religious than many ancient laws, they still decree that some legal violations merit more severe penalties or remedies, because certain bad acts imply a bad moral choice, as well as being violations of the law. This ongoing distinction in types of violations is especially important when the accused is a minister or religious worker.

Ministers and Moral Violations

Does an accusation against a minister of a violation that has both a "moral" and "legal" element have a more negative impact than if the accusation is a "legal" claim alone? Undoubtedly, yes. Consider, for example, how a minister might feel if he or she or the church they serve were sued by a party who had slipped and fallen on ice in front of the church building. The minister might be discouraged because of the financial threat posed to the church or frustrated because of the "both factor" of having to inform the church insurer and possibly pay higher premiums. But the clergy person's life and ministry certainly would go on.

What if parishioners suffered smoke inhalation from a fire in the church, when they could not immediately escape from the burning building because the minister had allowed some chairs to block the exit? The minister surely would feel terrible and might be viewed as careless or even foolish. But most still would not think of the minister as an evil person.

What, however, if the claim against the same minister was for sexual misconduct against a minor? For defrauding an elderly widow of her finances? Or for embezzling church funds for personal use? Even the thought of such accusations makes most ministers queasy. Such claims introduce an obviously moral dimension, whereas the earlier examples seem, as we have dubbed them, purely legal.

Moral claims against ministers are especially troubling because of the minister's place in the community. Historically, ministers and churches have been the custodians and dispensers of moral direction in our society. But religious communities and their leaders, at least in the public's eyes, also created the distinctions between selective bad acts. Thus, moral charges against ministers go to the heart of what they are entrusted with in their profession. Just as doctors are presumed to have a certain concern for their patients' health and police personnel are presumed to uphold the law, ministers are presumed to possess a certain degree of moral integrity and must set an example through their conduct.

If ministers create circumstances that cause physical or financial harm, a legal remedy such as money is available to the complainant. But if the claim is that a minister caused moral, psychological, emotional, or "spiritual" harm, how can that harm be remedied with money? Arguably, harm to those areas cause even greater injury if brought about by a minister, because clergy are the very ones who are presumed to nurture and protect those aspects of our lives. The upshot for modern ministers, then, is that lawsuits accusing them of moral as well as legal violations are often professionally devastating, even if not true. This book explores seven groups of such devastating lawsuits that can have major consequences, financial and otherwise, for ministers or their churches.

Sadly, such claims occur often enough to make many ministers (and the leaders of their denominations) buckle at the knees, give up without a fight, and close the church doors, even when the clergy have absolute or mitigating defenses to rebut such accusations. This destruction of a minister's vocation and livelihood may be unfair, particularly when a legitimate defense exists, or when the minister admits to the bad act and is willing to pay the price of retribution and repent. As in ancient times, our legal system still holds that the penalty should fit, but not exceed, the crime or wrongdoing. Ministers need to know where to turn to avoid such excessively damaging situations.

SHEPHERDS AMONG SHARKS

The beginning of the 1990s revealed a startling increase in the number and intensity of lawsuits against ministers and churches. Seminars where lawyers could learn to successfully sue clergy sprang up around the nation. These seminars have drawn hundreds, even thousands of attorneys.

One such seminar held in New York City in 1992, sponsored by the American Bar Association (ABA), addressed the topic "Tort Liability of Charitable, Religious, and Non-profit Institutions." Speeches at that event had such titles as "Visiting the Sins of the Fathers on the Church." An attorney who attended another such seminar in San Francisco reported that as a religious believer, the atmosphere was "sort of creepy." While other seminars he had attended rightly taught that clergy who have acted illegally should be held responsible for their wrongdoing, that seminar emphasized the large settlement amounts and verdicts available to lawyers who sued clergy and their denominations, conveying an image of blood being poured into shark-infested waters.

Media coverage also has confirmed the increase in legal problems for ministers and churches. The *Wall Street Journal* (WSJ) published an article titled "Churches, Ministers, Finding Themselves Hit by More Lawsuits," reporting that attorneys and officials from several denominations had seen a rapid increase in the number of lawsuits against their church leaders.[10] Several reasons were cited for the increase. Mark Chopko, general counsel for the National Conference of Catholic Bishops, noted that the public has realized that churches have insurance. Also, the courts have begun to award punitive damages (i.e., exemplary money-damage awards, often totaling many times more than the amounts otherwise paid to a successful complaining party, and insurers of churches and dioceses have paid millions in settlements and verdicts. The Roman Catholic Church alone was estimated to have paid approximately $400 million for lawsuits brought against the church.)[11] Finally, the increase in lawsuits is also due to society's loss of public reverance for authority figures, including ministers. The public is simply more willing to sue ministers and churches.

Since the early 1990s, the dividing lines have been more sharply drawn. While seminars which teach attorneys how to successfully sue clergy and churches have multiplied, books and seminars to educate defense attorneys on how to defend their clients against those lawsuits also have emerged. Many divinity schools and theological seminaries have responded by instituting courses on "ministry and the law" as part of their curriculum.

Perhaps most disturbing about the negatively developing relationship between clergy and the law is that each year, more accusations of the worst types of bad acts, moral and legal, are levied against ministers and churches. When the accusations are true, they cause inestimable damage in the lives of those parishioners and other ministers who trusted the wrongdoer. When they are false, they often still "succeed," because they extort money from innocent, yet accused ministers, by means of huge out of court settlements. Too often, even falsely accused ministers can afford neither the enormous defense costs nor the emotional stress associated with defending a case against them throughout an entire trial. Even when many cases are finished and a minister or church is exonerated, the damaging publicity permanently attaches itself to the accused and negatively affects ministries for years to come.

Many lawsuits against clergy are undoubtedly handled responsibly, presented sincerely and honorably, and are meritorious. Despite this, it is also clear that guilty or not, ministers have become large and desirable targets for many plaintiffs' attorneys and their clients. Whatever the merits and outcome, clergy, churches, and religious organizations in America appear to be on the defensive in the legal system. Although this news is disturbing and probably discouraging for many in ministry, it unfortunately distorts another important reality—the vast majority of ministers in America continue to benefit their churches and parishioners as sincere, responsible, hard-working servants!

A Remedy: Prevention Through Education and Avoidance

The Reverend Clyde Grogan, chairman of the Southern Illinois Association of Priests, in response to an interview by the Associated Press regarding sexual misconduct lawsuits against rural ministers, stated, "When one priest is good, we all benefit. When one is bad, we all suffer the consequences." His frustrated remark was accurate and also insightful, in that it implies a fact often forgotten amidst the recent surge in lawsuits against ministers. Clergy and churches accused of wrongdoing represent only a fraction of the thousands of those doing ministry around the nation and around the world. The majority of clergy in America, by far, continue to responsibly serve their parishioners and the community.

Despite the good that ministers and churches do in society, it appears likely that they will face more lawsuits and regulation in the future. Neither courts, commentators, nor legislatures have helped to clear up many confusing legal issues that presently face clergy. Until the law develops in many areas, or until immunity statutes are passed to better protect clergy under a variety of circumstances, the best remedy is prevention.

No one can stop anyone from filing a lawsuit, even if the suit has no merit and can be successfully defended. Nor can any minister (or lawyer, for that matter) know all there is to know about all the laws that may affect them. In every state, court opinions and new statutes change yearly.

But ministers can learn about the kinds of situations that often lead to lawsuits. They can understand the elements of specific legal claims that may be especially damaging to their ministries. Many of the moral and legal bases for claims often filed against ministers remain constant. Fraud, for instance, almost always has to do with certain fairly clearly defined forms of deceit. Malpractice claims always address whether a person operated within certain standards of care.

It simply makes sense that if ministers will raise their level of awareness and learn the basic elements that lie at the root of the lawsuits that can affect them most gravely, they will be better equipped to avoid those cirumstances that may lead to such lawsuits in the first place.

Law Basics

Many people may fully understand the detailed maze that lawsuits go through once filed, and that the United States Constitution offers certain rights and privileges to religious believers. However, those who are less sure of such general knowledge should turn to the appendix, which offers a brief introduction and a review of some of the basics about how lawsuits work in most American courts and the protections provided to religious believers and churches by the First Amendment.

CHAPTER 1

Fraud

The administrators and the satraps tried to find grounds for charges against Daniel in his conduct of government affairs, but they were unable to do so. They could find no corruption in him, because he was trustworthy.

DANIEL 6:4 NIV

Food gained by fraud tastes sweet to a man,
but he ends up with a mouth full of gravel.

PROVERBS 20:17 NIV

*O*ne Sunday morning after a church service in the late 1980s, I heard two parishioners discussing Jim Bakker's PTL Ministry scandal. Verdicts had recently been handed down against Bakker by a United States Bankruptcy Court and a United States Federal District Court. In hardy agreement, the two churchgoers lamented.

"It was just wrong what he did," said one.

"Yes. It was deceitful. It simply amounted to fraud," said the other.

In the law, *fraud* is a specifically defined type of *tort*. A tort is personal injury resulting from a civil wrong. Technically, the Bakker lawsuits were about more than just fraud claims. They were like many that involve the mishandling of ministry funds. These lawsuits often involve issues of negligent misrepresentation, undue influence, breach of contract, breach of fiduciary duty, breach of duty of care or of loyalty, wrongful diversion of funds, and embezzlement.

As my parishioners' conversation revealed, however, the public generally does not care about the specific legal nuances that make up fraud claims. Instead, the public simply understands fraud in ministry to be a minister's act that involves dishonesty, questionable business dealings, advantage taking, or less than full disclosure—all done in order to obtain something (usually money) that does not belong to the minister. As with all the legal claims that are the focus of this book, fraud lawsuits are especially damaging to ministers, because the public expects them to be impeccably honest.

In many ways, the public is right to lump many legal theories together and refer to them as fraud. Although a plaintiff can allege many of the legal theories mentioned above in a fraud lawsuit, all these theories can be discussed as fraud because they all address facts which amount to the same wrong—that is, deceitful acts for illegal gain.

It is important that ministers understand the essential principles of fraud. It is not necessary to learn each element and legal doctrine related to the subject. However, they do need to learn and shun the actual situations that may lead to fraud claims. By doing so, they reduce the likelihood of becoming involved in a fraud lawsuit. Best of all, if ministers understand the nature of fraud and then shape their ministry to avoid it, they will then shine in all dealings as witnesses and examples of the highest standard of the moral integrity to which they call others in the course of their ministry. This comports with the biblical directives given to ministers from the earliest days of Christianity,[1] and also with the standards by which the public vigilantly observes with an ever watchful eye.

FACT SCENARIO

Many fact scenarios could give rise to fraud claims against pastors and religious workers. These include the hiring and dismissing of employees, church business dealings, fund raising, and the solicitation of gifts for the minister or church. Specific elements of fraud law are not always identical in each of these circumstances. However, in many such circumstances, the legal principles remain the same and are not difficult to identify.

This chapter will discuss the fact scenario from one of the cases in which Jim Bakker was a defendant.[2] Jim Bakker's acts are, indeed, an extreme example, the likes of which most ministers will never commit. However, extreme examples have a tendency to help "clear the air." The Bakker case is instructive in explaining many of the legal concerns that may arise for ministers, and which could lead to several types of lawsuits that fall under the umbrella of what the law refers to as fraud.

FRAUD

Jim Bakker and the PTL Scandal

In 1974, James Bakker formed a corporation known as the PTL Ministries. The PTL stands for "Praise the Lord" and "People That Love." The PTL's activities soon expanded from its initial focus on televised religious broadcasting, and by the late 1970s, the group had begun construction on "Heritage USA," described by PTL officials as a Christian retreat center for families. The concept of the center became increasingly ambitious in 1983, when Bakker planned to enlarge the center by adding a vacation park called Heritage Village, which would include a 500-room Grand Hotel. Between 1984 and 1986, Bakker announced further proposals to extend the Village by constructing the Towers Hotel, fifty bunkhouses, and several additional facilities.

The PTL planned to finance these projects by selling lifetime partnerships. Eleven different partnership programs, ranging in cost from $500 to $10,000 were offered, eight of which promised benefits that included annual lodging in one of the Heritage Village facilities. In January 1984, Bakker began using the mail to solicit lifetime partners. From February 1984 through May 1987, broadcasts carried over the PTL Television Network and various other commercial affiliates were used in the solicitation. At least $158 million dollars was raised through the sale of approximately 153,000 partnerships with lodging benefits. Many "partners" drew on meager incomes to purchase those benefits in Heritage Village.

Bakker promised television viewers that he would limit the sale of partnerships, to ensure that each partner would be able to use the facilities annually. However, the partnerships were oversold. For instance, Grand Hotel partnerships were to be limited to 25,000, but 66,683 were actually sold. In addition, relatively few of the funds solicited were used to construct the promised facilities. In fact, only the Grand Hotel and one bunkhouse were actually completed. Instead, Bakker used partnership funds to pay operating expenses of the PTL Ministries and to support a lavish lifestyle. This extravagant living included gold-plated fixtures and a $570 shower curtain in his bathroom, transportation in private jets and limousines, an air-conditioned tree house for his children, and an air-conditioned doghouse for his pets. This combination of overselling of partnerships and diverting of partnership proceeds meant that the overwhelming majority of partners never received the lodging benefits they were promised.

In response to these activities, on December 5, 1988, a grand jury indicted Bakker on 8 counts of mail fraud, 15 counts of wire fraud, and one count of conspiracy to commit fraud. The trial began on August 28, 1989, and lasted five weeks. The jury found Bakker guilty on all 24 counts; the court sentenced him to 45 years imprisonment and fined him more than $500,000.

Bakker and his attorneys appealed the conviction. The Fourth Circuit Appellate Court affirmed the conviction on the fraud counts, but remanded Bakker's case to the lower court for resentencing; the Appellate Court found that the trial-court judge had based Bakker's 45-year sentence explicitly on his personal religious principles, rather than upon the law as applied to the facts of Bakker's case.

Ultimately, Bakker's conviction of the 24 fraud counts was affirmed, but the hefty 45-year sentence was significantly reduced. He served four and a half years in a minimum security federal prison before being released to serve out the rest of his sentence in a half-way house in Asheville, North Carolina.

THE LAW REGARDING FRAUD AND DECEIT

When most people refer to "fraud," they usually are thinking of what is known as "common law fraud." However, under numerous legal theories, such as embezzlement, undue influence, or breach of fiduciary duty, a defrauded party might also sue a minister to recover damages resulting from allegedly fraudulent acts. The following section explains common law fraud, then gives a brief explanation of some of these other legal theories.

Common Law Fraud

The law regarding fraud in most states is based upon "common law," or state law articulated by judges in prior precedent-setting legal cases. Fraud sometimes also is called "intentional misrepresentation" or "deceit." In almost all states, to establish a conviction of fraud, the following elements must be proved:

1. The alleged wrongdoer must make a false representation;
2. the false representation must be of a material past or present fact;
3. the false representation must be intentionally made by the defendant;
4. the false representation must be made with the intent to induce another party's reliance on the misrepresentation;
5. the false representation must cause actual reliance;
6. the reliance by the defrauded party must be justifiable or reasonable;
7. damage must result from the reliance upon the false representation.[3]

A plaintiff must prove those specific elements in order to obtain a fraud conviction or verdict (in a civil suit) in most states. Some states have described fraud more broadly, to include a variety of means by which human beings may gain an advantage over another by false suggestions or by suppression of truth. These means may include surprise, trick, cunning, and any other unfair way another can be cheated.[4] This definition explains fraud as including all acts that deceive, including omissions and concealments calculated to deceive, and which result in damage to another person.

Case law regarding fraud reveals that people will go to great lengths and use remarkable creativity to deceive others for illegal gain. Cases have included deception by what people say, as well as by what they fail to say. Fraud may be the suppression of truth or the suggestion of what is false; it may be accomplished by speech, silence, innuendo, a look or a gesture, or by publication. Fraud may be done by a single act or by a combination of circumstances designed to deceive. Fraud may be personally carried out, or agreed upon through a conspiracy and carried out by many. Attorneys who deal with fraud cases learn first-hand that human beings have an astounding ability to deceive not only others, but also themselves.

Key Issues in Common Law Fraud Cases

The success of common law fraud cases usually hinges on certain pivotal issues, which are worth reviewing here in some detail.

1. *Materially* False Representation. The defendant's misrepresentation must be *material*. In other words, a defendant must misrepresent a fact that is of critical importance to the deceived party. For example, presume that a defendant is selling a building to a plaintiff, and in the process convinces the plaintiff that the sky is green, not blue. Later, after the plaintiff purchases the building, the plaintiff sues the defendant, claiming that he was defrauded when he found out that the sky is really blue. The plaintiff probably would lose, because the color of the sky was not material to the sale of the building.

If, however, the defendant represented to the plaintiff that the building was in excellent structural condition, but in reality the foundation was cracked, then the plaintiff would have sufficient grounds for suing the defendant for having defrauded him in regard to a material fact in the sale of the building—namely, the crack in the foundation.

2. Duty to Disclose *All* Information? As noted, fraud claims often arise in the context of business transactions. The law in most states is that there is no general duty to disclose material facts or opinions in most relationships involving business transactions. However, numerous exceptions exist to this general rule. If two parties are in a fiduciary relationship with one another, then there would be a duty to disclose material facts, or facts that one party knows, should know, or which the other party would reasonably want to know.[5] Also, if one party is selling something (particularly real property) and knows that the potential buyer is unaware of and cannot reasonably discover material information about the transaction, the seller may be under a general duty to disclose the undiscoverable facts.

For example, if First Church is selling a building to Second Church, and First Church officials do not tell Second Church that First Church was built on a toxic landfill, the First Church officials may later be accused and found liable for defrauding Second Church in the sale of the building.

Similarly, if one party states something that he reasonably knows will deceive or confuse another party who is relying upon the speaker's statement, then the speaker will be under a duty to inform the listener of the true facts. For instance, if Pastor Bob, in selling his van to the church, tells the church that it is like a new vehicle, but in reality he knows that when he bought the van, the odometer had been turned back, then Pastor Bob may be guilty of having defrauded the church if the church purchases the van, later has problems with it, and then sues Pastor Bob for fraud.

3. Intent, Knowledge, or Reckless Disregard for Truth. The *intentional* element of fraud requires that a plaintiff prove that a defendant made a *knowingly* false representation. The plaintiff may also do this, however, by showing that the defendant's representation was reckless, regarding its truth or falsity. For example, if at a church fundraising function, the Reverend Sales, without having looked at a profit and loss statement, enthusiastically states that last year's profits were $100,000, and people purchase bonds for a church building project based upon his reckless representation, the "intentional" element of fraud probably will have been satisfied.

This example is similar to the way Jim Bakker wrongly raised funds for PTL Ministries. In selling partnerships for the Grand Hotel, he promised to limit those sales to 25,000. In reality, he oversold the partnerships, selling 66,683—far more than the facility actually would accommodate.

After his trial, Bakker stated that he never had intended to deceive anyone. This may be true. Nevertheless, his reckless disregard for the truth of his promises to limit the sales was ultimately enough to convict him on several counts of fraud.

4. Inducing Others to Rely. The "intent to induce reliance" element of fraud simply means that a party must have intended to induce another person or persons to act, or to refrain from acting, in reliance upon a false statement. For example, if church officials sell bonds in order to raise funds for a new building and induce the purchasers of bonds to purchase them, based upon faulty or inflated financial reports about the ability of the church to pay back the bonds, those church officials will likely be viewed as having intended to induce reliance through the false financial statements.

Liability for fraud may exist even where a party induces a third party through a false financial statement. For instance, if the pastor passes out the false financial statement in order to sell bonds to the congregation, and then someone in the congregation shows the statement to a third party who purchases the bonds based upon the false representation, the third party could also have a claim for fraud against the pastor.

5. Actual Reliance. The inducement must actually cause the allegedly deceived persons to *act* upon their reliance. For example, a person may pay money for a goods or service and rely upon its supposed value. A person actually relying upon a false representation may also *forebear* from doing something. This also can be actual reliance. For instance, if a buyer does not improve a leaky roof because he was told the roof was new, and later the roof leaks and ruins the interior of a building, the buyer's forbearance from fixing the roof would be considered reliance upon a false representation that the roof did not need to be repaired.

6. Justifiable Reliance. The reliance of an injured party must be *justifiable*. As noted above, this is related to the materiality aspect of fraud. As a practical matter, the reliance of an injured party on false representations is almost always justified. Only where the facts are obviously false may such reliance not be justified. Courts generally do not want to impose a duty upon plaintiffs to investigate the truthfulness of a lying party's representation of the facts.

7. Actual Damages Required. Finally, as is true with any personal injury lawsuit, actions for fraud will succeed only if actual loss (usually monetary) results from reliance upon the false statement.

Other Claims Related to Fraud

The previous description of common law fraud, or intentional misrepresentation, exists in some form or other in almost every state. However, other legal theories also may be the basis for lawsuits against ministers who have deceived another party or the public. Undue influence (and to some extent breach of fiduciary duty) focus more on the deficiencies of the victim than on the deception of the actor. Undue influence also usually addresses questionable gifts, donations, or bequeaths, and these will be addressed in chapter 7. Following is a brief explanation of several other legal theories closely related to fraud.

Negligent Misrepresentation. Negligent misrepresentation is virtually identical to common law fraud, except for the fraudulent actor's state of mind. While intentional misrepresentation involves either deliberate or reckless conduct with regard to the truth or falsity of a communication, negligent misrepresentation exists where a party is negligent as to the truth or falsity of a communication, and it is foreseeable that another party will rely upon that communication.

For example, a minister carelessly prepares a statement which inaccurately reflects the financial status of a church, and then obtains a loan from a bank based on the erroneously prepared financial statement. The minister may be liable for damages resulting from the negligent misrepresentation, if the church is later unable to repay the loan. The other elements of causation, justifiable reliance, and damages are analyzed in the same manner as intentional misrepresentation.

Breach of Duty of Care and of Loyalty. Claims for breaches of the duties of care and loyalty often accompany fraud claims. The board members of both nonprofit and profit corporations have a duty under the law to act in good faith, in the best interests of the corporation, and with the prudent care that an ordinary person in the same circumstances would use. The same board members are also under a duty to act loyally toward a corporation. These concepts are typically referred to as directors' or officers' duties of care and of loyalty. If directors or officers act below the standards of other prudent and reasonable officials in like circumstances, they may be liable for resulting damages. Some church organizational structures are such that ministers and/or church lay leaders are directors and officers of the church board. As such, they are under these duties of care and loyalty.

A United States Bankruptcy Court which oversaw the bankruptcy of PTL Ministries also addressed the liability of the directors and officers of PTL.[6] Jim Bakker was both an officer and a director of PTL. Based upon his actions as described in our fact scenario, the bankruptcy court concluded that Bakker had breached his duties of care and loyalty in a several ways. First, he failed to inform the board members of the true financial position of the corporation and to act accordingly. Second, he also failed to supervise other officers and directors in the PTL Corporation. Third, he failed to prevent depletion of the corporate assets of PTL. Finally, he violated the prohibition against self-dealing when he diverted PTL funds, which had been raised for partnerships in the Grand Hotel at Heritage Village, and spent those funds on his own opulent lifestyle. Similar diversion of church or ministry funds by a minister, director, or officer of another ministry could result in similar legal liability for those officials.

Securities Law Violations By making false representations or misleading statements about the financial status of the church in order to sell church securities, ministers violate federal securities laws under the Uniform Securities Act.[7] The Federal Securities Act and the Uniform Securities Act prohibit any offer, sale, or purchase of any security facilitated by any device, scheme, or artifice to defraud. The sale of any security must be impeccably handled, and even if they are not directly involved, church officials should pay close attention to any such sale.

The Uniform Securities Act permits a defrauded investor to recover interest, costs, and attorney's fees, all in addition to the purchase price of any security fraudulently sold. In addition, criminal penalties may be imposed, up to $5,000 in fines and three years imprisonment for willful violations of the antifraud provisions. The Federal Securities Act of 1933 provides civil remedies, as well as criminal penalties, up to $10,000 in fines and five years imprisonment for willful violations.[8]

DEFENSES

A minister or religious worker accused of fraud or a related claim may have an effective defense under the First Amendment of the United States Constitution, based on the person's entitlement to the free exercise of religion. It is not always clear, under the First Amendment, whether a court may inquire as to whether an individual is sincerely advocating a religious doctrine or is falsely professing something for fraudulent purposes. Obviously, as the Bakker case illustrates, ministers can be held responsible for fraudulent acts. However, in some instances, ministers and religious workers have responded to fraud claims by denying that their acts were in any way fraudulent, asserting that any allegedly false statements they had made were actually sincerely held religious beliefs.

A landmark case in this regard is *United States v. Ballard.*[9] In that case, the defendants, the Ballards, were charged with using the mails to obtain money by fraud. Edna and Donald Ballard claimed that they had been divine messengers of "St. Germain," the "spirit" of their son, Gary Ballard. The Ballards raised funds for their ministry, representing themselves as divine messengers and teachers, able to heal many diseases, including many medically incurable ailments. The indictment against them charged that they "well knew" that their representations were false and fraudulent. The Ballards maintained that they were sincere in their religious assertions.

The *Ballard* case went all the way to the United States Supreme Court, which held that the constitutional guarantees against the establishment of religion and the assurance of free exercise of religion prohibited the government from inquiring into the truth of the Ballards' religious beliefs. The Supreme Court determined that to hold otherwise would allow a trial for religious heresy. But while the Court held that no court could inquire into the falsity of a religious belief, it did not rule on whether a court can inquire whether the defendant honestly held the belief. One Supreme Court justice held that to allow an inquiry into a defendant's good faith in asserting a belief was not materially different from scrutinizing the belief itself. Neither of the inquiries, according to that justice, should be allowed by a secular court.

Two final points have emerged regarding fraud claims against religious leaders and institutions since the *Ballard* opinion. First, the court's inability to inquire into religious beliefs does not prohibit legislatures from outlawing certain actions based on those beliefs. For example, the government could ban collecting money from the public to cure AIDS by a means other than accepted medical procedures. Such a law would not necessarily question the fundraiser's religious beliefs, especially if the same laws regarding fundraising applied to all citizens. (However, there still may be a question as to whether this legislation would violate the free-exercise rights of believers who adhere to faith healing.)

Second, the *U.S. v. Ballard* case did not address the question of whether a person seeking a benefit from the government because of religious beliefs can be questioned by the government. For example, if people claim conscientious objection to avoid participating in a military draft, they still could be tested by both the draft boards and the courts. However, the court cannot inquire into the truth or falsity of the belief itself, based upon the *Ballard* decision. Therefore, ministers retain at least a defense of sincerely held religious beliefs when confronted by allegations of fraud in lawsuits, even if the sincerity of that belief may be questioned.

PREVENTIVE MEASURES

Fraud, in its common law form, is an intentional tort over which we have control, much like many kinds of sexual misconduct. As in the case of sexual misconduct, if you are tempted, or are considering the perpetration of a fraud, get help! You haven't done the act yet. Bring yourself into accountability by telling a trusted friend your thoughts. Remember, the act of fraud not only constitutes civil wrongdoing, but in certain forms also amounts, in most states, to a crime punishable by imprisonment.

Since fraud claims allege that a person acted with a deceitful state of mind, there is only one absolute way to determine whether fraud actually occurred. The defendant must admit the deceit. Because this rarely happens, and since no judge or jury is able to read a person's mind, the law often determines whether fraud occurred based upon *indicia* of fraud. In other words, the court asks whether certain factors or facts were present in the situation in question to *indicate* that a defendant was acting fraudulently.

Reviewing, understanding, and avoiding these *indicia* of fraud is the most helpful and practical way to avoid claims of fraud being levied. Drawing upon typical *indicia* of fraud considered by many courts, the following paragraphs offer helpful hints to avoid any appearance of fraud:

---

1. **Be attentive to the age of the persons with whom you deal.** Courts often examine whether the person who was allegedly defrauded was of a particularly vulnerable age. If the plaintiff is a much older person and may have lacked the sensibilities and awareness of the situation, or if the plaintiff is particularly young and may have been naive or unable to understand the gravity of a situation, then the court is more likely to determine that the defendant committed fraud.

2. **Avoid gifts made under unusual circumstances.** Courts often will review whether gifts made to a minister or church were made

---

under circumstances wherein the donor was particularly vulnerable to the suggestions of clergy. For example, if a gift is made by a person who is dying or very ill, a court may presume that fraud was present. If persons were so ill that they lacked the mental awareness truly necessary to determine whether they wanted to give a gift, fraud may be present. Ministers should avoid soliciting gifts under such circumstances. If parishioners ask that a minister be present while they are dying and want to make a gift under such circumstances, ministers should be sure that others are present at such meetings.

3. Consider the health of parishioners with whom you deal. Like the previous examples, if a person's health in any way impinges upon the ability to understand a gift, a business decision, or other transaction entered into with a minister or church official, a court may determine that fraud was the basis of the transaction. The transaction may be avoided or undone, with damages awarded to the victim. Thus, again, ministers should ensure that others are present at such meetings.

4. Does a fiduciary relationship exist? As has been noted, if a fiduciary relationship exists between a minister and another party, wherein the minister has an advantageous position over that party in some way, or the party has placed special confidence in the minister as a matter of law, there will be a heightened scrutiny of the acts of the minister. For example, if a minister fails to disclose a fact about a particular transaction made with a person who trusts and relies upon the minister, then it may be determined that the minister may have acted fraudulently. In all relationships when dealing with a sick, elderly, or emotionally distraught person, or a child, ministers should act with extreme care before proceeding, disclosing all facts the other party may want to know in any business dealing or transaction.

5. Do not isolate parishioners from their relatives, friends, or guardians. Persons committing fraud typically want to keep their acts and victims in the dark. Their actions are performed in secrecy. Therefore, if a minister denies allegations of fraud, and the facts reveal that he or she attempted to isolate the alleged victim of fraud from relatives, friends, guardians, or others who may have instructed the alleged victim to act otherwise, a court may determine that such facts indicate that the minister acted fraudulently. All ministers would do well to carry out their church dealings and transactions with at least some measure of accountability to and openness with others. It is understandable that not all church business dealings should be known to the public at large. Some business matters require privacy. Nevertheless, rarely should a minister's business dealings be so private that they include no other party, observer, or consultant than the party with whom the minister is dealing. Openness creates natural accountability, and it also provides the appearance of propriety and good faith in all dealings.

6. **Encourage all parties to a transaction to seek independent and disinterested advice.** If a minister or religious worker enters into a transaction which another party later claims was fraudulent, a court will more likely believe fraud was involved if the minister failed to encourage that party to seek independent advice. If the minister encourages the person to seek independent counsel in writing, this will go even further to dispel any likelihood of fraud, demonstrating that the minister acted with honesty and integrity.

7. **Be sure that all parties are allowed to exercise "free will" in a business dealing (even if you are a Presbyterian).** In order for any contract to be legal and valid, one of the requirements is that the parties act freely and deliberately in choosing to enter into the contract. If a minister uses coercion or any conduct intended to overpower or unduly influence another in a contract or transaction, that minister may be accused of fraud, undue influence, duress, or another related claim. Again, clergy would do well to encourage others with whom they deal or transact business on behalf of the church to seek independent advice. They should conduct their business dealings among others who can verify that everything was done in honesty.

8. **Create *indicia of honesty.*** Church and religious workers can creatively consider other ways in which openness, honesty, free choice, and full disclosure for all parties will regulate all transactions and occurrences in their church and ministry. For instance, consider devising, in consultation with the church staff and board members, a list of *indicia of honesty!* It might be determined that all church expenditures over fifty dollars must be verified by at least two people. Or all staff members approaching parishioners or others outside the church for financial gifts must agree to divulge their intention prior to doing so. Such a list could be included as part of the church's policy statement and will further safeguard against questionable dealings by creating a milieu of openness and integrity.

On October 6, 1989, the *Charlotte Observer,* commenting on the prosecution of local televangelist Jim Bakker on charges of fraud and conspiracy to commit fraud, stated:

In soliciting donations from his flock, a preacher may promise eternal life in a celestial city whose streets are paved with gold, and that's none of the law's business. But if he promises an annual free stay in a luxury hotel on Earth, he'd better have the rooms available.

The media seem to delight in reporting incidents of fraud, or even alleged fraud, in ministry. In the Bakker case, the media seemed to take a special delight in reporting every detail of the demise of his ministry. Perhaps the press had perceived Bakker as flamboyant and self-righteous prior to his legal troubles. Or perhaps it was simply that the press loves a scandal, and fraud in ministry makes for one of the best scandals. Whatever the case, the message of the Bakker case was clear. If ministers or religious workers are associated with fraud claims, it will have a devastating effect on their ministries.

Honesty in religious business dealings is not merely expected, it is historically rooted. Even in Old Testament times, King David of Israel associated principles like integrity, honesty, voluntary willingness in giving, and loyalty to God with religious fundraising. In First Chronicles 29:16-18(NIV), David thanked God for faithfulness in providing the funds that he and the Israelites were able to give toward the building of the Temple:

> O LORD our God, as for all this abundance that we have provided for building you a temple for your Holy Name, it comes from your hand, and all of it belongs to you. *I know, my God, that you test the heart and are pleased with integrity. All these things have I given willingly and with honest intent. And now I have seen with joy how willingly your people who are here have given to you.* O LORD, God of our fathers Abraham, Isaac and Israel, keep this desire in the hearts of your people forever, and keep their hearts loyal to you (emphasis added).

Ministers and religious workers sometimes appear surprised, and even indignant at the suggestion that they need to avoid fraud claims in their ministries. Most ministers are not devising overt and sinister conspiracies to defraud their congregations. However, their small acts of *omission* are more troubling than than those of *commission*. Each of us has the subtle ability to deceive ourselves, and occasionally to turn a blind eye to absolute honesty and integrity when there is an advantage in it for us. The problems are caused by the statements that are *not* made by a clergy person in a business dealing or a negotiation, the seemingly insignificant information that is *hidden* from parishioners or board members, or the directed funds that were *not exactly* directed toward their intended source. All these scenarios, while done with relative innocence, too often legally explode in the faces of ministers in ways they never imagined. Thus, ministers are urged to be *straightforward* in all their dealings, to avoid ever being accused of anything except exemplary integrity.

CHAPTER 2

Defamation

Lying lips conceal hatred, and whoever utters slander is a fool.

PROVERBS 10:18

Sticks and stones can break one's bones, but names—at least in the adult world—can destroy one's reputation, get one fired, and ruin one's professional life. This is the theory behind the legal claim of *defamation*. Defamation is a claim for damages to a person's reputation, character, or occupation, resulting from false and disparaging "publications" made against him or her. Defamatory words are often described in the law as those that tend to expose one to public ridicule or contempt. Defamation is sometimes described as a damage to the dignitary, as well as the economic interests of a person. Historically, if the "publications" were made orally, the defamation was called *slander*. If they were in writing, the defamation was called *libel*. Use of the specific terms *libel* and *slander* has diminished in recent years, in favor of the more general term, *defamation*.

Ministers can commit defamation. They can also be the victims of defamatory remarks. This chapter is concerned with the former—ministers as defendants because they have allegedly committed defamation. This is not to say that it is unimportant when ministers are defamed. It is extremely important. Ministers' reputations are often their most valuable asset. The key focus of this book, however, is situations in which ministers may *themselves* be accused of conduct that is viewed as both legally and morally wrong.

Being accused of committing defamation—that is, of broadcasting a false and disparaging statement about another person—may be grossly damaging to the reputation. It not only calls the minister's character and judgment into serious question, but it can destroy hard-earned public trust that often takes years to establish. Unwary ministers can commit defamation in some seemingly innocent ways, and with the best of intentions. For this reason, individuals involved in all aspects of religious work should understand the elements underpinning defamation law and learn to avoid the kinds of situations that may lead to defamation lawsuits.

FACT SCENARIO

Many famous ministers have been involved in defamation lawsuits before the public. Jimmy Swaggart and numerous other defendants were sued for defamation and related claims by another minister.[1] The suing minister claimed that Swaggart and the other defendants had wrongly publicized the minister's ouster to others outside the church, who had no legal or moral business knowing about the church's discipline against him. Jerry Falwell sued *Hustler Magazine* and its editor, Larry Flint, for a lewd cartoon published in that magazine, depicting Falwell committing sexual acts with his mother in an outhouse.[2]

These high-profile cases drew great public attention. However, many defamation cases are filed based on occurrences in average churches situated in average American towns. The following example is virtually identical to an actual publicized lawsuit and typifies the kinds of scenarios that can occur in a multistaff church.[3]

Accusing Fellow Staff Members of Adultery

Jan Johnson grew up in a hometown with strong ties to its neighborhood church, St. Matthew's. Over the years, Jan's mother had been both a volunteer and an employee at St. Matthew's. Jan, too, had spent many of her formative years participating in the numerous activities St. Matthew's offered its youth.

As Jan became older, she volunteered as an administrative assistant for a church youth group called Teen Life and, later, for a traveling drama group called Acting Christian. Both groups were directed by the associate pastor, Pastor Rowe. Jan worked very closely with Pastor Rowe, including traveling as a counselor with him and the other members of Acting Christian for four months a year.

After graduating from college, Jan was hired at St. Matthew's by the recently promoted Director of Youth Ministry, Pastor Wood. Although Jan's position, Associate Director of Youth Ministry, was salaried, she also continued as a volunteer for Teen Life and Acting Christian. Thus, she worked for both Pastor Rowe and Pastor Wood.

While Jan was away on a church-sponsored trip to the Holy Land led by Pastor Rowe, Pastor Wood entered her office to look for a file he needed. There he discovered a file marked with the initials of both Pastor Rowe and Jan. Curious, he opened the file and found personal letters and notes from Pastor Rowe to Jan.

Although these contained no specific romantic references, they fed Pastor Wood's growing suspicion that Pastor Rowe and Jan were engaged in a sexual relationship. Pastor Wood, claiming that he intended to protect Pastor Rowe's wife, showed the letters and notes to Mrs. Rowe. He also offered specific details of when and where he believed that the rendezvous of the two had occurred. Pastor Wood also showed the letters and notes to a staff assistant to the senior pastor of St. Matthew's.

A few days after informing Mrs. Rowe, Pastor Wood repeated his suspicions to Jan's mother. Again, he suggested specific details, along with his opinion that Pastor Rowe and Jan might never return from the church excursion.

However, they did return, and after Mrs. Rowe talked with her husband, she told Pastor Wood that she did not believe her husband's relationship with Jan was sexual. Pastor Wood accepted Mrs. Rowe's understanding of the incident and retracted his allegations. In order to encourage healing, the church then initiated counseling sessions, during which Pastor Wood stated that he "no longer believed" that the relationship between Jan and Pastor Rowe was sexual. He *promised,* at one of the counseling sessions, to keep his prior suspicions confidential. He also apologized to Jan and to Pastor Rowe for the pain he had caused them.

Despite Pastor Wood's promise, some time after the counseling sessions, he *again* repeated his original accusations to members of the congregation who were active in Acting Christian. In no time, the other members of Acting Christian, and most of the congregation, learned of Pastor Wood's claims against Jan and Pastor Rowe. Soon, Jan began receiving unsettling phone calls and mail from church members, and a short time later, the church formed a special committee which dismissed Jan from employment at St. Matthew's.

Jan was subjected to scorn in her church and neighborhood, and was unable to find a job commensurate with her skills. She then sued Pastor Wood for defamation of character and invasion of privacy. She also sued St. Matthew's, claiming that the church had "ratified" Pastor Wood's accusations by dismissing her.

After a two-week trial, a jury awarded Jan nearly $230,000 in general damages, and an additional $107,000 in "punitive" damages. Although both the youth pastor and the church appealed the jury's decision, a state appeals court upheld the jury's verdict.

THE LAW OF DEFAMATION

In order to state a legal claim of defamation, a plaintiff must prove at least the following elements:

1. The defendant used defamatory language (defamatory statements historically were presumed false under the law, but the defendant could rebut the claim by proving the statement was true).

2. The defamatory language was "of or concerning" the plaintiff. This means that a reasonable reader, listener, or viewer would understand the plaintiff to be the target of the defamatory language.

3. There was a "publication" of the defamatory language by the defendant to a third person or persons.

4. There was actual damage to the reputation of the plaintiff.

In cases where the defamatory publication refers to a public figure or involves a matter of public concern, two additional elements must be proved as a part of an actionable case (i.e., a case that is allowed to proceed through the courts):

5. There was fault (or "malice") on the defendant's part. *Malice* means a defamatory statement made with the *knowledge* that the statement was false, or a *reckless disregard* for the truth or falsity of the statement.

6. The defamatory language was materially false.[1]

In the actual lawsuit on which the St. Matthew's example is based, the court acknowledged that a plaintiff who is a "public figure" (such as a pastor) sues someone for defamation must prove that the defendant acted with fault or malice. As noted, malice means that the defendant either knew that the defamatory statements were false, or that he uttered them with reckless disregard to their truth or falsity. In the real lawsuit, the court concluded that the Director of Youth Ministry ("Pastor Wood") indeed acted with malice, because he repeated statements which he had already acknowledged were not true.

It is worth reviewing each element of defamation law to understand how that law applies in other specific instances of defamation.

1. Defamatory Language. Defamatory language is language which tends to adversely affect one's reputation or occupation. It often denigrates one's honesty, integrity, sanity, or virtue. It may be established by explicit statements or by innuendo. For instance, a minister may erroneously report in a church newsletter that a parishioner has been cleared of sexual misconduct charges. The minister's report may be considered defamatory if the parishioner was never accused of sexual misconduct charges. Even pictures, satires, drawings, dramas, or other such nonverbal statements may be defamatory.

Statements of alleged fact may always be defamatory, because they usually appear more believable and definite to listeners. For instance, if a minister says, "My associate has slept with fifteen men in the last week," it sounds more definitely ascertained than if the minister had said, "In my opinion, my associate is permiscuous." Statements of opinion, however, will be defamatory only if they appear to be *based* on facts, *and* if an explicit accusation of those facts would be defamatory. For example, if a minister says, "I don't think the church secretary can be trusted with the offering money," this statement may imply a personal knowledge of dishonest conduct by the church secretary. It therefore might be actionable as defamation. Whether a publication is fact or opinion depends upon the nature and circumstances of the publication. Jerry Falwell's legal claim against *Hustler Magazine* for defamation failed, in part because the court determined that a cartoon would not be perceived by the reasonable reader as a factual claim about Reverend Falwell.[5]

2. "Concerning" the Plaintiff. A plaintiff in a defamation case must establish that a *reasonable* reader, listener, or viewer would understand the plaintiff as the target of the defamatory statement. In some cases, for instance, an individual may use defamatory language in reference to a group. In most states, if the individual defames all members of a small group, each member may establish that the defamatory language was damaging to him or her by establishing that he or she is a member of the group. If, however, the defamatory language refers to all members of a large group, typically the members of that group are not allowed to attempt to establish that they were the targets of the defamatory language. The more specifically the defamatory language is directed toward one person or group of persons, the more likely a court is to allow a suit to proceed against the defendant who allegedly made the statements.

3. "Publication." A publication is simply a communication to a third person or group who understands it. If an angry pastor suddenly blurts out defamatory statements in German to his board members about a specific parishioner, and no one understands, the publication requirement may not be satisfied. But a defamatory publication that is understood by only a single person may be actionable.

Ordinarily, a plaintiff need not show that the defendant acted with evil intent. It suffices if one acts with an intent to publish a defamatory communication. A minister may falsely report in a church newsletter that a parishioner was acquitted from a sexual misconduct charge. Even if the minister neither knew nor had reason to know that the plaintiff had never been accused of sexual misconduct, so long as the publication is established, the minister may nonetheless be liable for defamation. It is the intent to *publish*, not the intent to *defame*, that is required for a defamation lawsuit.

How many defamation lawsuits could an injured party file if 500 copies of a magazine print the same defamatory remark? One! Most courts hold that each time a defamatory statement is repeated, there is a separate recoverable violation for defamation damages. In most American courts, however, this does not mean that if 500 copies of a church newsletter defame one person, that person may sue for 500 separate instances of defamation. The "single publication rule" would treat the initial

4 6

publication of numerous copies of the church newsletter as a single act of defamation.

4. *Damages* Resulting from Defamation. Three kinds of damages are often considered in defamation suits: general, special, and punitive damages. General damages in defamation cases are often presumed in the law. They need not be proved by the plaintiff. General damages are intended to compensate the plaintiff for the general injury to his or her reputation caused by the defamation. Certain kinds of defamatory statements do *presume* a compensable injury. For example, slander to one's business or profession, a defamatory statement that a person has committed a crime, or personal unchastity are often considered the kinds of slander for which injuries and recompense is presumed.

Special damages are damages which a plaintiff must specifically prove to a court, by demonstrating that the plaintiff suffered a particular financial loss to the plaintiff's reputation as a result of the defamatory statement. Such loss typically does not include injured feelings, loss of friends, or personal humiliation. Instead, special damages usually include the loss of a job, customers or clients, an advantageous business relationship, or a prospective gift or inheritance. If a plaintiff can prove that he or she suffered a loss of these things and can place a value on them, the plaintiff may be awarded amounts for these special damages.

Punitive damages are exemplary and sometimes are awarded to punish the defendant for knowingly and intentionally making defamatory statements against the plaintiff.

5. Fault. Historically, liability for defamation was often automatic if a defamatory statement was made against a person, whether the defendant acted negligently, recklessly, or with intent to injure. In the last few decades, however, the United States Supreme Court has rendered decisions requiring that the plaintiff prove fault in certain cases. The degree of fault to be established depends upon the type of plaintiff—that is, whether he or she is a public official or figure, as compared to a private citizen. This is important for ministers, since ministers often are considered public figures because they voluntarily inject themselves into the public eye or become prominent community figures for certain issues.[6] Conceivably, a minister may even become a public figure through no purposeful action of his or her own, although this is considered exceedingly rare.[7]

A court may require fault in a defamation suit by one minister against another, especially if the plaintiff minister is considered a public figure. The rationale behind this rule is that if a person chooses a profession which naturally exposes him or her to the public eye, that person must also expect greater public criticism than the average private person.

What kind of fault do courts require that a public plaintiff show? A public plaintiff must show "malice" in order to succeed and to recover damages in a suit for defamation. *Malice* is defined as a defamatory statement made with the *knowledge* that the statement was false, or a *reckless disregard* for the truth or falsity of the statement. In other words, the defendant must *know* or *strongly suspect* that a statement is false. Where a defamatory statement is in regard to a nonpublic person, there is less concern about freedom of speech and the press. Private individuals are more vulnerable to injury from defamation because they have fewer opportunities for rebuttal than does a public person. For this reason, public plaintiffs must prove malice, and private persons usually do not need to prove malice to succeed in defamation suits. Many states, however, require private persons to prove at least that the defendant was negligent.[8]

6. Falsity. Historically, courts presumed that defamatory statements were false. Defendants would then be required to defend themselves against the allegation of defamation by proving that the allegedly defamatory statements were true. More recently, however, the United States Supreme Court has rejected the presumption of falsity in all cases. Particularly in cases where the plaintiff is a public figure or official (as ministers are sometimes defined), the plaintiff may have the burden of proving that the alleged defamatory statement was materially false.[9]

As we will see in chapter 6, even if an allegedly defamatory statement is *true,* a minister who makes a disparaging statement about another person still could be liable for the statement, under the legal theories of *intentional infliction of severe emotional distress* or *invasion of privacy.*[10]

DEFENSES

Numerous defenses exist for ministers accused of defamation. The defenses usually fall under one of two broad categories—

"absolute" and "qualified" defenses. (These are also sometimes referred to as absolute and qualified *privileges* to make statements which may otherwise be deemed defamatory.) Some of the most common absolute and qualified defenses against defamation are as follows:

Absolute Defenses

1. Consent. If a person consents to a defamatory communication, that person will not later be allowed to claim that he or she was defamed. For instance, if a staff member asks a minister for a recommendation for another job, and the minister indicates that the letter will be negative in nature, that person cannot ordinarily later complain if the letter is, indeed, negative. As with all types of legal consent, the consent must be *voluntary* and *knowing*, in order to be a complete defense.

2. Truth. If a statement is true, virtually all courts simply do not consider it defamatory. As a matter of public policy and First Amendment rights, courts are extremely hesitant to impede the dissemination of truthful information, even if it is denigrating. In the last few decades, some courts have allowed parties to succeed on the theory of "invasion of privacy." (See chapter 6.) This legal theory holds parties liable when they have made statements which, although truthful, contain extremely private, personal facts, and public disclosure of them is unreasonable and shocking. Our personal and private sexual habits with our spouses, for example, may be truthful, but they are certainly not everyone's business.

3. Legal Proceedings. Judicial and legislative proceedings, such as those made before a judge, jurors, an attorney, and witnesses, or remarks made by federal or state legislators in their official capacity, are absolutely privileged. Even if statements made in those contexts would otherwise be defamatory, anyone making statements there, including ministers, have an absolute defense to subsequent defamation claims against them.

4. Communications Between Spouses. Typically, communications from one spouse to another are generally treated as being absolutely privileged.

Qualified Defenses

In other contexts, ministers have qualified privileges to make statements that otherwise might be considered defamatory. Such entitlements are considered "qualified defenses" or privileges to free speech.

1. Theological or Doctrinal Statements. One of the contexts in which defamation suits have been filed against ministers concerns a person being disciplined by a church for immorality, based upon biblical or theological reasons. Clearly, such discipline has biblical precedents.[11] Many denominations within Christendom continue to maintain elaborate disciplinary codes as part of their controlling church documents. They use these codes as directives in disciplining ministers, church officers, and church members for moral and procedural violations of biblical and church norms.

Because of the sincerely held religious motivation for such discipline, churches typically are entitled, under the First Amendment free exercise clause, to carry out this discipline with impunity, despite making statements that would otherwise be defamatory against a person being disciplined.[12]

Church officials who carry out these disciplinary actions may not *always* enjoy this qualified defense. First, if legal malice is proven by a plaintiff, a minister or church official may not use this defense. In other words, if in a church disciplinary proceeding, a person makes a disparaging statement that he either knew was false or made it with reckless disregard for its truth or falsity, that person cannot later defend against a defamation action by raising a First Amendment defense. Second, statements made in church disciplinary actions must be made only to those church officials or members whom it concerns or who are entitled to hear it.

In *Gorman v. Swaggart,* the court held that while it was powerless to interpret religious doctrine in church disciplinary actions, it did not give church officials cart blanche to make biblically based moral accusations against a person outside the context of their denomination.[13] Conversely, communications made from one minister to another on a subject in which both have a similar interest, have been held *not* to be defamatory.[14]

2. Self-Defense. If a person is defamed, many courts will permit that person to respond to the defamation in a way that *itself* may be defamatory. However, those defensive comments must be limited to the charges made against the person. For example, if Pastor Smith is accused of adultery by Pastor Jones, Pastor Smith may reply by saying, "Pastor Jones is a liar and always has been." If Pastor Jones sues Pastor Smith for defamation, Pastor Smith will likely be able to defend his statement that Pastor Jones was lying about his defamatory remark of adultery. However, Pastor Smith may not have the same defense regarding his assertion that Pastor Jones has *always* been a liar.

3. False Reports at Public Proceedings. Although truthful statements made before legal and public hearings are absolutely privileged, ministers who make false or inaccurate statements at the same proceeding will not be able to raise that defense in a later defamation claim against them for their remarks.

Mitigating Factors

Certain matters, while not actually defenses against an accusation of defamation, can be considered by courts and juries to mitigate damages for which a defendant may be liable in a defamation lawsuit.

1. Retraction. If a party, immediately after the publication of a defamatory remark, retracts the statement, a court may consider that retraction to show a lack of actual malice.

2. Anger. If a person is provoked, becomes angry, and then makes a defamatory statement, the court may consider that in determining damages.

3. No Ill Will. If defendant ministers could show that no ill will existed when they made otherwise defamatory remarks, this evidence may mitigate the damages against them. Defendant ministers in such a case may be allowed to prove the source or basis of their defamatory statements.

PREVENTIVE MEASURES

Ministers would do well to keep the following key points in mind, in order to avoid the likelihood of being sued for defamation:

1. Speak Well of Others. As a general matter, ministers should not make public remarks that disparage the reputation or esteem of others. This may sound simple, but it is not simplistic. Ministers are in the "people business." They frequently have the occasion and need to speak about the lives of others, often publicly. Also, because people frequently come to ministers in times of crises, ministers often know the worst details about people's lives. Consciously avoid, even in subtle ways, divulging these details in contexts that may prove damaging to others.

2. Avoid Occupation Assassination. Those in ministry must be particularly cautious to avoid saying anything about others that could negatively affect their occupations or professions. Accusing another minister, for example, of willful deceit, a greatly confused mind, or gross immorality, all have been deemed defamatory.[15] Other professionals in the church, such as doctors, attorneys, counselors, teachers, youth workers, and the like, all rely heavily upon the soundness and purity of their professional reputations. Ministers must avoid ever making gratuitous or careless statements, even to an audience of one, which may damage those reputations.

3. Cautious Publishing. All in ministry should avoid disseminating, in flyers, bulletins, posters, or other publicized materials, information that could injure another's reputation and is not necessary for the general church public to know. Avoid publishing the dismissal of church staff or the results of disputes, particularly when they concern information about specific people. Pastors should avoid stories from the pulpit that may even remotely disparage a parishioner. This is true even when the parishioner is not named, because it later could be claimed that reasonable hearers would have known the identity of the person.

4. Be Private. Sometimes ministers have legitimate conversations in which they need to discuss negative aspects of another person's life. Often these conversations are well-meaning and intended to help the other person, but later the minister learns that his or her statements about the person were untrue. Such statements may be defamatory. Thus, ministers should exercise great care in maintaining privacy and carrying on such conversations only with those who have a direct interest and are in a position to help the subject of the conversation. Some conversations that ministers have, such as those with spouses, are privileged, and they can feel free to discuss things in those contexts. Even privileged conversations, however, if discussed too loudly in contexts in which they are overhead, may later be deemed defamatory publications. Maintain a high degree of privacy when discussing delicate matters about the lives of others.

5. Keep Church Matters In-house. Otherwise defamatory comments made in the context of church disciplinary proceedings or between church officials, all of whom have an interest in the discussion, are privileged discussions, not ordinarily considered defamatory by courts. However, these discussions must remain in-house, and should be discussed only by those who need to know the information for official ecclesiastical or theological reasons.

6. Keep Church Matters Accurate. All statements made in the context of church disciplinary actions, or in other church contexts in which negative remarks are made about a person, must be made truthfully and accurately. Ministers and church officials should not guess, estimate, or presume any negative facts about someone before they state those facts verbally to others. Any false statement, whether made intentionally or not, may later be deemed defamatory, and may expose anyone who made the statement to tremendous liability.

7. Retract Defamatory Remarks Immediately. If a minister believes that he or she has made a defamatory statement, it should be immediately and publicly retracted.

8. Truth May Not Be Enough. Even if a statement about another person is truthful, a minister should be careful that the statement is not unreasonably or shockingly private. See chapter 6, Invasion of Privacy.

The Levitical Law recognized the seriousness of defamation, sandwiching prohibitions against it between laws against perversion of justice and endangering a neighbor's life (Lev.19:15-16). The apostle Paul similarly recognized slander as a sin characteristic of a severely broken world, listing it with other serious vices like murder and hatred of God (Rom. 1:29-30). In almost everyone's ministry, it will be necessary at certain times to discuss negative aspects of others' lives or characters. It is impressive, however, to see ministers who skillfully address such delicate issues discretely, diplomatically, tactfully, and in a Christlike way. All in ministry would do well to heed Paul's directives to his young fellow ministers Timothy and Titus, to let even their exemplary speech reflect the purity and soundness of their faith and actions (I Tim. 4:12; Titus 2:7-8). Such speech not only has the effect of maintaining a biblical, Christlike faith, but also protects one from the very serious and damaging pitfalls of being accused of defamation in a court of law.

CHAPTER 3

Child Abuse

And whoever welcomes a little child . . . welcomes me. But if anyone causes one of these little ones who believe in me to sin, it would be better for him to have a large millstone hung around his neck and to be drowned in the depths of the sea.

MATTHEW 18:5-6 NIV

Jesus did not typically threaten his disciples into obedient submission. The above text from Matthew certainly contained some of Jesus' strongest language about reprisals that would result from engaging in a specific kind of bad act— namely, taking part in causing a child to sin. Jesus' directives were not unfounded. His words were buttressed by strong laws in the Old Testament against incestuous sexual abuse and exploitation of children (Lev. 18:6-16, 23-24; 19:29).

The growing problem of abuse of children (and, in some cases, of the elderly and the mentally ill) is one of the single most volatile issues for all those in ministry today. This is not to say that it is the most frequent problem for ministers. But the public usually views most harshly any deliberate violations or even mistakes that involve the lives of children. If ministers are even accused of abuse against children, their careers in ministry are usually finished.

This chapter is about two kinds of legal violations that ministers can be accused of in their interactions with children: (1) legal liability because the minister sexually molested a child; (2) legal liability for failing to report known instances of child abuse by others. We examine each in turn, beginning with child abuse committed by ministers.

FACT SCENARIO

Bill Martin was only ten years old when he first met the Reverend Darby. Reverend Darby was an associate minister in charge of junior- and senior-high youth at the Lutheran church Bill attended, and Bill was active in both youth groups.

Fifteen years elapsed between the time Reverend Darby left Bill's church to work at another parish and the next time they saw each other. Darby was at his third church appointment by that time, with almost twenty-five years of ministerial experience. But instead of meeting in church, he and Bill met in a courtroom. Bill had filed a lawsuit, claiming that the pastor had sexually abused him during the five-year period Darby was his youth minister. Bill's claims were based on legal theories of intentional infliction of emotional distress, assault, clergy malpractice, and breach of fiduciary relationship.

Reverend Darby denied all Bill's claims, stating that he never had engaged in sexual improprieties of any kind throughout his entire ministerial career. He hired an attorney, who emphasized that Bill had no physical or corroborating evidence or testimony to support his claims.

In addition to the civil suit, Bill had approached the state prosecutor, requesting that the state press criminal charges against Reverend Darby for the alleged past sexual abuse. Although the state prosecutor would not agree to immediately press charges against Darby, he did agree to fully investigate the validity of Bill's claims.

CHILD SEXUAL ABUSE LAW

The previous scenario addresses both criminal and civil child sex-abuse laws as follows:

The Criminal Case Against Reverend Darby

Sexual violations committed by an adult against a minor often are described as "child abuse." Child abuse may take a broad variety of forms. It may, for instance, involve cruelty to a child's physical, moral, or mental well-being. It may involve a sexual

5 5

attack by an adult, which may or may not amount to rape. Child abuse, in most states, is a criminal offense, and depending upon the facts alleged in a particular case, may be punishable as a misdemeanor, requiring a fine or penalty, or as a felony, punishable by a prison sentence. Recent child-abuse laws in many states have increased penalties for proven acts of child abuse. In any event, if an individual is accused and convicted of an act of child abuse, especially of a sexual nature, that person will suffer not only social disdain, but also will be slapped with criminal penalties.

In many cases involving religious workers and child sexual abuse, the difficult question is not whether a person should be punished if he or she has abused the child. The more difficult issues for most prosecutors are threefold. First, is the statute of limitations a barrier to prosecuting the suit? In other words, is the case too old to prosecute? Second, when cases are very old, can the prosecutor muster sufficient evidence to prove that a defendant is guilty beyond a reasonable doubt? Finally, if it is determined that the case can be brought by the prosecutor and that a defendant/minister can be convicted of child sexual abuse, what sentence should the court impose upon the person?

The Statute of Limitations   Simply because a case of child sexual abuse is old, even very old, does not mean that a prosecutor will be barred from prosecuting the case. First, some states allow a long statutory time period (that is, 10 years from the date of the offense), in which minors can sue if they are sexually mistreated.[1]

In other states, the statute of limitations begins running once the case is reported to a law enforcement official.[2] If the above scenario was in a state which had such a statute, once Bill reported the case to a law enforcement official, the prosecutor then has the time allowed under the statute of limitations (often from two to eight years) to file the case against the minister.[3]

Other states require that the statute of limitations in child sexual abuse cases begin running during a certain period after the alleged victim has reached an age of majority.[4] In other words, if a state's age of majority were 18 years, the alleged victim would have a stated amount of time (for example, five years) after he or she turned 18 in order to report the case to a law enforcement official. If the case was not reported, then the victim and the prosecutor would be barred from bringing the case against the alleged assailant.

Finally, some states' satutes regarding the time limitation in which to sue for alleged child sexual abuse offer a combination of the above rules, allowing the victim to bring the case from the latest of any of the above time periods.[5] Thus, one can see that if the above scenario occured in many states, the prosecutor would not automatically be prohibited from bringing the case against Reverend Darby.

Problems of Evidence   The evidence problems are closely related to the problems associated with statute of limitations. Statutes of limitation exist for a reason. If too much time passes after an alleged wrongful act has occurred, memories will fade, evidence will disappear, witnesses move away or die, and records are destroyed. Thus, legislatures have enacted statutes of limitations to encourage cases to be brought quickly by parties who have been wronged.[6]

Despite the existence of statutes of limitations, many child abuse cases still are not filed until long after the alleged abuse has occurred, because the children are often very young when the incident happened and they were unable to verbalize the abuse. The testimony in such cases is, therefore, often incomplete, unclear, or in some way unreliable. Thus, some states have more relaxed evidentiary laws which make it easier for state prosecutors to obtain and get into court evidence that would not otherwise be allowed in an adult case.[7]

In the above scenario, once the state prosecutor has agreed to investigate the case, she will do so in a variety of ways. She may, for instance, go directly to Reverend Darby to ask his version of the story. The prosecutor may examine church records, to see if there was any indication of child or sexual abuse by Reverend Darby at any other time in his ministry. The prosecutor is likely to talk with other individuals who were in the youth group with Bill, asking if they knew of any aberrant behavior by Reverend Darby when he was the youth leader. No matter what the state prosecutor does to investigate the case, however, fifteen years can be a long time, and many state prosecutors investigating such situations would find it difficult to sufficiently establish the evidence needed to convict a defendant like Reverend Darby beyond a reasonable doubt of a child sexual crime.

However, even if Reverend Darby is not prosecuted and convicted of child sexual misconduct, a prosecutor's investigation against him may be exceedingly damaging to his reputation as a minister. Reverend Darby has wisely hired an attorney to represent him, even during the prosecutor's investigation, in order to strategically and effectively respond to the state prosecutor, whether she decides to file charges against him or not. In most states, a prosecutor needs only probable cause to support filing charges, even though proof beyond a reasonable doubt is required for a conviction. If the alleged victim is still a minor, the abuser will often be reported to a state or county child protective services agency. This agency may conduct a separate investigation and may seek protective orders from the juvenile court, prohibiting unsupervised contact between the alleged offender and other children—a prohibition which *no* minister could effectively explain to his or her congregation.

Problems of Sentencing   If the case is not barred by the statute of limitations, and if the prosecutor finds sufficient evidence to bring the case against Reverend Darby to trial, a judge or a jury may decide that Reverend Darby is guilty as charged. Many prosecutors and courts, however, have had a difficult time fashioning sentences against child molesters and abusers who have committed only one or a few offenses many years ago. It is expensive to incarcerate a person in any state or federal facility. Also, many prison systems are full, and courts have a strong policy for filling them with only the worst offenders, those who pose an ongoing danger to society.

Many argue that once a person is a child abuser, he or she always runs the potential of abusing other children in the future. Thus, child abusers should be incarcerated or suffer heavy criminal penalties, no matter how long ago their last act of child abuse. However, even if this is true, courts still face the practical realities of having to rid the streets of imminently dangerous murderers, violent rapists, drug dealers, and terrorists. If it appears to a court that a person has committed an act of child sexual abuse in the past, but somehow has rehabilitated him or herself so that he or she no longer poses an immediate threat to society, that court may release the defendant into society without a prison sentence, imposing a fine and/or a probation upon the convicted child abuser instead.

CHILD ABUSE

The Civil Suit Against Reverend Darby

Even if Bill fails in his attempts to get the state prosecutor to press charges against Reverend Darby, the pastor is still not out of the woods. In the previous example, Bill has also filed a civil lawsuit against the minister. In the civil suit, the burden of proof is not as heavy as in the criminal case. In order to prevail, Bill must prove only by a preponderance of the evidence (that is, based upon the evidence, that it is more likely than not), rather than beyond a reasonable doubt, that Reverend Darby committed the alleged acts of child abuse. Otherwise, many of the same problematic issues addressed in the criminal case must also be addressed in the civil lawsuit.

The Statute of Limitations   First, there may be some question as to whether Bill has filed the lawsuit beyond the statute of limitations. Typically, in lawsuits for damages resulting from child sexual abuse, the statute of limitations usually runs from the time of the abuse itself. However, because children are often deemed incapable of or extremely reluctant to report sexual abuse against them, a variety of theories have been created as exceptions to the customary limitations.[8] The three main theories which delay the running of the statute of limitations on civil damages for child sexual abuse are as follows: (1) the "discovery" theory, (2) "tolling" of the statutory period during the child's minority, and (3) "equitable" (or fairness) arguments raised by the plaintiff, asserting that it would be unconscionable or unfair for the defendant to simply get away with the child sexual abuse on the technical grounds of plaintiff's failure to file the lawsuit in time. We will deal with each of these in turn.

1. The "Discovery Theory." The discovery theory is sometimes successfully argued by plaintiffs who claim to have been abused as children, but who are bringing the lawsuit years after the alleged abuse, and after the statute of limitations for filing the suit has run. These plaintiffs often assert that they did not actually know that they were sexually abused until many years later. Plaintiffs may argue this, for example, if they did not know what sexual abuse was at the time. Or, that they only recently discovered that they were sexually abused by an adult defendant when they were unconscious or asleep. Sometimes plaintiffs have contracted sexually transmitted diseases some years after being

abused and, thus, argued they did not discover their child sexual abuse until years after it had happened. Still other plaintiffs have argued that their memories were psychologically repressed, so they did not have a conscious awareness of having been sexually abused by a certain defendant until the memory somehow surfaced. All of these arguments are used to extend the time in which plaintiffs are otherwise allowed to bring child sexual abuse lawsuits without dismissal.

Courts have differed widely on whether they should allow the discovery rule to toll statutory limitations in which the plaintiff has to bring a lawsuit. The success of the discovery rule argument is highly fact specific to each case and also depends upon the jurisdiction in which a plaintiff is arguing for the rule.

2. Tolling of the Statutory Period During Minority. Some jurisdictions have simply legislated into their state laws an exception to the general rule that the statute of limitations begins running once the personal injury occurs. Typically, in such states, a person who has been abused as a child has until some specified time after they reach an age of majority (usually anywhere from 18 to 21) to bring their lawsuit against the defendant abuser.[9] In many respects, the statutes simply codify the discovery rule discussed earlier.

3. Equitable Arguments. Equitable arguments sometimes are allowed by courts to extend a statutory period of limitations if no other legal authority exists in the form of a statute or a prior case. Courts may allow these arguments if, despite a general rule to the contrary, an application of that rule would be patently unfair.

For example, many who abuse children put the children under duress by telling them that if they tell anyone about the abuse they will injure or even kill the child or a loved one. Other child abusers may lie and defraud the children, making them think that it is perfectly normal that the acts of child abuse are taking place. In either of these instances of duress or fraud, a court might say that the child abuser may not now argue that a child waited too long to file the lawsuit, thus allowing the child abuser to get away with the abusive act.

Even these arguments may fail, however, if the plaintiff waits an excessively long time to file the lawsuit. For example, in a case called *Schmidt v. Bishop* (779 F.Supp. 321 [1991 S.D.N.Y.]), a woman more than 40 years old alleged that she had been abused by a clergyman/counselor at the age of 12. She also argued that she had been under duress not to tell anyone about the abuse. Despite her claim of duress, the court dismissed her case, based on the defendant's assertion that the statute of limitations had run. The court reasoned that it was extremely doubtful whether any reasonable juror could find that the plaintiff was under constant legal duress for 31 years. In addition, during that time, the plaintiff had lived a half continent away from the defendant. Such circumstances made it impossible for the court to believe that the plaintiff's claim of duress had merit.

Cases which involve the three previously mentioned exceptions to the general statute of limitations rules should send some very clear messages to religious workers tempted to engage in, or actively engaged in, child sexual abuse. First, even if a minister sexually abused a child many years ago, he or she still may be held legally accountable for that abuse. Second, because children are considered more vulnerable and impressionable than adults, some courts will go to great lengths to see that child abuse victims receive justice. Finally, even if a victim is not allowed to proceed with a civil case because of the statute of limitations, a state prosecutor still may be able to pursue charges against the abuser for the same occurrence or other occurrences of child abuse.

Problems of Evidence   Bill also may have the same evidentiary problems as a state prosecutor in finding supporting and corroborating evidence for his claims of child sexual abuse. Again, Bill has an advantage over a state prosecutor in that Bill need not prove his claims "beyond a reasonable doubt." Bill's standard proof in a civil case is a "preponderance of the evidence," meaning that if Bill uses evidence that is of greater weight or is more convincing than the evidence offered by Reverend Darby (51 percent or more), Bill should win his case.

Remedies   Sentencing of defendants occurs only in criminal cases. Civil cases are said to devise "remedies" to address damages resulting from one's civil injury against another. If Reverend Darby is found guilty of the alleged molestation against Bill, the minister cannot take back the bad acts. He can, however, be forced to pay monetary damages, even exemplary damages called "punitive" damages, for his bad acts against Bill. Some courts may also attempt to stop Reverend Darby's continued employment in ministry; or a court may direct Reverend Darby to get counseling. Other creative remedies are available to courts, as well.

Even if Reverend Darby is innocent, he and his attorney must seriously consider whether they want to proceed toward a full-blown trial on the merits of this case, allowing the case to be reported by the local media. Such publicity in itself, could permanently damage Reverend Darby's reputation as a minister.

What if Reverend Darby admitted that he had some physical contact, but tried to defend himself, claiming that he did not sodomize or rape Bill? Under the laws of many states, such a defense would achieve little for Reverend Darby. "Molestation" or "sexual abuse," within the meaning of many state laws, means even *touching* the genitalia, buttocks, or breasts of a child under a specified age.[10] Thus, Reverend Darby must offer a more substantial defense, or must attempt to settle this case out of court; otherwise Bill will most likely proceed to trial with his civil lawsuit and win an amount of damages determined by a judge or jury.

PREVENTIVE MEASURES

Ministers surely should not, as a biblical matter, stop hugging or loving children, simply because they are afraid of lawsuits. Physical pastoral care for children was an explicit directive of Jesus to his disciples.[11] However, ministers should consider the following:

1. **Work with children in groups.** Religious workers should avoid working alone with children for long periods of time.
2. **Love children, but in public.** Appropriate and loving touching, hugging, or kissing of children should occur in public places around other adults.
3. **Do background checks on child-workers.** Churches hiring ministers or other religious workers should conduct thorough background checks on prospective employees, especially if they will be working with children. These investigations should include telephoning or writing past employers or the local police in an applicant's past geographic locale to inquire about any questioned sexual behavior.

4. Keep records. Keep a journal or other record to document all activities with children, especially if they are done alone with kids, such as counseling.

In addition to these specific suggestions, ministers should seriously consider the two lists at the end of chapter 4, "Preventing and Addressing Sexual Misconduct in the Church" and "Damage Control After False Accusations."

The flurry of child sexual abuse lawsuits against clergy may also ensnare some ministers who are not at all guilty. Some of these suits may be sincerely filed, but factually wrong. Others may maliciously intend to extort money from ministers and/or their religious organizations, because the plaintiffs know that the clergy will be unable to handle the public and financial stresses associated with such lawsuits. Avoiding any and all scenarios that might look suspicious or lead to any claim of child sexual abuse by a minister is imperative. State and local agencies dealing with child abuse or children often offer practical and helpful information on how to avoid such scenarios. However, common sense and circumspect behavior seem to be the least expensive and most valuable kinds of advice.

CHILD ABUSE REPORTING LAWS

When reporting others' abuse against children, ministers often find themselves in the untenable position of being publicly and legally damned, whether they report the suspected incidents or not. If well-meaning clergy fail to report such incidents, they often are viewed as callused or careless toward children. Conversely, if they report an incident and later find that the facts were other than they were told, they are viewed as meddling home wreckers who should have minded their own business. Ministers are faced with the dilemma of whether to tell or not to tell.

Every state in the United States has some form of child-abuse reporting laws. Each state also has legislation mandating that states cannot compel ministers to disclose, in a court of law, information told to them in confidence in their capacity as ministers or spiritual advisors. These often are referred to as "privileged communication statutes." States differ on the extent to which a given state's child-abuse reporting statutes apply to ministers. Each state statute also may differ in the way it effects the privileged communication statute in that state.

This section attempts to inform ministers about child-abuse reporting and privileged communication laws, and how ministers, by complying with these laws, might avoid some of the worst kind of damage to children and to their own reputations.

FACT SCENARIO

In almost every state, child abuse is defined as including both sexual misconduct and physical abuse. In many states, child-abuse reporting is required of a broad variety of those who work with people, including ministers. In some states, even when under the language of the statute, ministers are not explicitly required to report suspected incidents of child abuse, they will be required to do so, insofar as they fit the definition of another professional who works with people and is required to report— for instance, a "social worker."

Often, when those who work in ministry but are not formally ordained learn of a suspected incident of child abuse, they may think they are exempt from having to report it because of their unordained status. This is an unwise assumption. The following scenario is taken from an actual case in Washington state. This case reveals that in some states, and under some circumstances, working in ministry while not being ordained is exactly what will expose a minister to liability for failing to report a known or suspected incident of child abuse.

Not Speaking When Spoken To[12]

All three ministers—Reverend Hartley, Mr. Mensonides, and Mr. Motherwell—were employed as paid religious counselors at the Community Chapel. Only Reverend Hartley was actually ordained at the time of the events in question. During the course of counseling, three separate parishioner families told the three counselors of incidents of alleged abuse.

A woman counselee told Reverend Hartley that her husband had sexually mistreated their daughter. Reverend Hartley had subsequently counseled both the husband and the daughter about the allegations, in an attempt to reconcile the family. A second woman told Mr. Mensonides that her husband had beaten their sons, ages four and seven. Mr. Mensonides talked to the older son about the allegations. A third woman told Mr. Motherwell that her husband was sexually abusing their eight-year-old daughter and showing violence toward the whole family. None of the counselors reported these incidents to authorities within 48 hours, as was required under the state's statutes that control child-abuse reporting.

There appeared to be no question that each counselor had a deep concern for the counselees and the children who had been victims of the alleged abuse. At issue, however, was whether the ministers had handled their knowledge of the abuse lawfully, under the state's child-abuse reporting law.

That law did not explicitly include a requirement that "ministers" or "clergy" report. In fact, sometime earlier, the Washington state legislature had amended the statute to omit the term *clergy*, which previously had been included as one of the groups of professionals required to report child abuse. The statute in effect at the time of the ministers' alleged failures to report, however, read in relevant part:

> When any practitioner, professional school personnel, registered or licensed nurse, social worker, psychologist, pharmacist, or employee of the department [of social and health services] has reasonable cause to believe that a child or adult . . . has suffered abuse or neglect, he shall report such incident, or cause a report to be made, to the proper law enforcement agency.[13]

The Washington statutes further defined "social workers" as:

> anyone engaged in a professional capacity during the regular course of employment in encouraging or promoting the health, welfare, support or education of children, or providing social services to adults or families, whether . . . as an employee . . . of any public or private organization or institution.[14]

The trial court found all three counselors criminally guilty of failing to report the suspected child abuse under the statutes, a violation considered a gross misdemeanor. Each received a deferred sentence with one year's probation and was required to complete a professional education program concerning the ramifications of sexual abuse. Mr. Motherwell was ordered to pay a $500 fine.

All three ministers appealed the convictions. The appellate court upheld the convictions of the two unordained minister/counselors, Mr. Mensonides and Mr. Motherwell. The court reasoned that their activities clearly fit the state-law definition of "social workers," who were required to report suspected child abuse. The appellate court rejected the defense of those two defendants that under the First Amendment, they were entitled not to report the alleged child abuse. None of the defendants had claimed that their religion required them to keep confidential all information learned in counseling ssessions. Thus the court found that to require the defendants to report suspected child abuse did not prevent them from counseling their parishioners or practicing their religion.[15]

Only Reverend Hartley's conviction was overturned on appeal, because he was an ordained minister. There was no applicable privileged communication statute protecting communications made to him by the parishioners in his capacity as a minister. However, Reverend Hartley successfuly argued that the state legislature had amended the child-abuse reporting statute not to include clergy in the list of professionals required to report alleged abuse. The court agreed that clergy would not have been removed from the list if the legislature still intended to require them to report. The court further acknowledged that as a matter of public policy, if the government required clergy to report all instances of abuse, abusers would be dissuaded from ever confessing to their clergy, in order to repent and bring healing to their lives.

THE LAWS ON REPORTING ABUSE OF CHILDREN

Child abuse reporting statutes are determined by each state's legislature. In some states, these laws also require the reporting of abuse of the elderly and the mentally ill. Reporting laws are often to be read in tandem with a state's clergy-penitent statute. Perhaps more than any other aspect of the laws discussed in this book, it is imperative that everyone, whether ordained or not, who works in any kind of ministry, ask any attorney in their state to explain their state's child-abuse reporting requirements and privileged communications laws! Violations of these laws occur far too easily, and the penalties for them are far too serious simply to ignore.

In addition to seeking the advice of an attorney, ministers would be wise to acquire a general understanding of many commonly asked questions regarding child-abuse laws.

What is the legal definition of child abuse?

Most states provide a specific definition of child abuse. It usually includes physical and sexual abuse, physical and emotional neglect, or any other maltreatment reasonably calculated to lead to such abuse or neglect. The age definition of children or minors varies from state to state. In many states, a minor is a person seventeen years old or younger.

Must ministers report child abuse in every state?

Ministers are not required to report child abuse in every state. There are essentially four kinds of child (and in some cases, elderly) abuse reporting statutes which, in some way, require ministers to report such abuse:[16]

1. Some states require that any person—including clergy—who learns of suspected child abuse must report.[17]
2. Some state statutes specify that clergy must report.[18]
3. Some state statutes imply that clergy must report suspected child abuse.[19] Most states permit, but do not require, any person who suspects or knows of child abuse to report such cases to authorities.[20]
4. Some state child-abuse reporting statutes exclude clergy from the list of personnel who must report.

The implication is that clergy are exempt from the requirement to report child abuse. The policy behind these kinds of statutes, of course, is to encourage free and open communications between the public and the clergy, to discuss incidents of child abuse in the hope of finding help and stopping the abuse. Even in states where this kind of statute exists, however, ministers may be viewed as fitting under the definition of another listed party who must report, as in the Community Chapel case above. Thus ministers should never assume that they are not required to report incidents of suspected child abuse until they speak with an attorney in their state.

What are the consequences of wrongly reporting or not reporting?

Child-abuse reporting statutes typically immunize those who wrongly report abuse in "good faith"—that is, with reasonable basis and good intentions. A person who intentionally and falsely reports child abuse, however, may be subject to civil, and even criminal liability in many states.

If a person who is required to report an incident of child abuse fails to do so, that person is subject to criminal as well as civil liability in many states. Most states classify a failure to report child abuse as a misdemeanor punishable by up to six months to one year in jail and a fine of from $500 to $1,000. In addition to criminal penalties, a statute also may hold a violator civilly liable.

What must one report?

Ordinarily, statutes require that one report the name of the child allegedly abused, if known. The person should also report his or her whereabouts, the name and address of the parents or guardians, the nature and extent of injuries, any evidence of previous injuries, and the identity of the person allegedly responsible for the abuse.

How does a state's clergy-penitent privileged communication statute affect a requirement that a minister report child abuse?

All states have statutes designed to protect confidential communications (or "religious confessions" in some states) from being forcibly disclosed in a court of law or other legal proceeding. This means that if a person tells a minister something in the course of pastoral counseling or receiving spiritual advice, a court cannot generally force the minister to come into court or another legal proceeding, such as a deposition, and report what the person told the minister.

Despite the existence of this privilege, it has some limitations in most states. First, most states hold that communications to ministers are protected only if the ministers are ordained, licensed, or commissioned in some formal way. Second, the communications typically must have been told to the ministers in their role as clergy. Some states require that in order for a communication to be privileged, it must be told to a cleric by a person who is confessing the problem or genuinely seeking spiritual help. Thus a parishioner who is bragging, rather than repenting about an act of child abuse or another crime, has not divulged a privileged communication. Finally, the penitent usually holds the privilege. This means that unless the penitent consents to a privileged communication being divulged, a minister cannot divulge it. In some states, there must be a mutual agreement to divulge the communication before it can be told.

How can states provide both a privileged communication statute for clergy, and also statutorily require them to report child abuse?

States handle the interaction of these two types of statutes in various ways:

1. Some state child-abuse reporting statutes nullify all confidentiality privileges, thus providing confidentiality for all communications with a minister, except those of child abuse, which the minister must report.[21]
2. Some states nullify all privileges except the attorney-client privilege. In these states, ministers who learn of alleged child abuse can confidentially seek the advice of an attorney. But the minister still eventually will be required to report the child abuse.[22]
3. Some states draft into their child-abuse reporting law a privilege protecting ministers from being required to testify about child abuse or any other clergy-penitent communication in a court of law, yet the ministers still are required to report the child abuse to state agencies or police, who will investigate the report.[23]
4. Some states specifically nullify the clergy-penitent privilege, and unequivocally require that such communications be reported.[24]

Ministers should remember that even if their state child-abuse reporting statute does not nullify their privileged communications with parishioners, they still may be required to report child abuse. A minister may learn of alleged abuse in a way not anticipated under the statute—for example, by overhearing an abusive incident or hearing it through a third party. Also, the privilege protects information from being coerced only as testimony in courtrooms and legal proceedings. Ministers still may be required to tell police or state child-care officials about the suspected abuse.

DEFENSES

Ministers who learn of an alleged child abuse case, but do not report it and later face charges under a child-abuse reporting statute may typically raise several defenses:

1. The state's statute did not require them to report the incident in their case. A minority of state statutes define child abuse as a wrongful act against a child "done by a parent or guardian." Thus, in those states, if a teacher, youth-group leader, or another party abuses a child, the minister may not be legally required to report the alleged abuse—even in a mandatory reporting state. However, they still may feel a moral obligation to report.

2. The communication from which the minister learned of the abuse was privileged. If a clergy-penitent communication statute existed in a minister's state, the minister may not be required to report the alleged abuse.

3. A First Amendment Defense. The Washington court in the case previously cited above determined that the First Amendment did not protect the two indicted ministers from penalties for statutorily failing to report child abuse. In great part, this was because the ministers did not claim that their religion required them to keep confidential all information they learned in counseling. If they had made such a claim, the reporting requirement in that state could have coerced a direct violation of their religious tenets. This probably also would have been a violation of their First Amendment rights.[25] The First Amendment may be a successful defense, then, for some religious communities in some states, but it should not be looked to by ministers as a sure defense for withholding child abuse information in all cases.

PREVENTIVE MEASURES

Child-Abuse Reporting Laws

Ministers should consider the following measures to assure compliance with child-abuse reporting laws in their state:

1. Seek the advice of an attorney in your state to explain the state's laws. There probably is no legal problem discussed in this book that requires the advice of a local attorney more than the issue of child-abuse reporting. Not only are these laws state-specific, but they also often require a legal explanation of how they interact with the state's clergy-penitent privileged statutes.

Ask an attorney in your church or one who is an acquaintance. It is critical that ministers know and understand the child, elderly, and mentally ill abuse reporting statutes in their states. Once church staff members learn about these laws, they should stay apprised of any legal developments in such areas, through annual seminars or ongoing consultation with a local attorney. Ministers are exposed to the problems which trigger child-abuse reporting statutes far too frequently to ignore them.

2. Encourage communicants to report themselves, with your support. Ministers who are approached by a confessing child abuser or by one informing the minister of abuse by another, should encourage the communicants to report the abuse themselves. If the communicant is the abuser, the self-report not only will dispel later confidentiality problems, it also will aid in the confessional, repentance, and healing process of the abuser. Self-reporting ensures the confessing abuser's sincerity and follow-through in seeking healing. If an informant is a spouse or related in some other way to the abuser, encouraging the communicant to report will help that person stop acting like a victim and start taking action to stop the abuse. Ministers who encourage such reports also should agree to stand by the communicant as he or she reports—in some cases, literally. This will show the extent to which the minister is genuinely interested in the abuser's welfare and ultimate healing.

3. How can ministers report child abuse and yet maintain confidentiality? There may be a way. Ministers may sometimes feel compelled to report a suspected incident of child abuse. But they may not want to be exposed as the source, for fear that will lessen their effectiveness in further helping the affected family, or in helping other parishioners who may come to the minister for confidential counsel.

A practical way around this problem may be for the minister to go to an attorney, then make an anonymous telephone call from the attorney's office to report the child abuse to the proper authorities. The attorney will then complete an affidavit attesting that the minister made the report, in case anyone later accuses the minister of failing to report the known case of child abuse. The affidavit can be placed in a safe place or a safety deposit box for future reference if needed. Thus the child victim is cared for, the minister's legal obligation is fulfilled, and the minister's reputation for maintaining confidentiality is spared.

Some problems may exist even with this proposed solution. First, if the minister lives in a state where the information he gave was protected by the clergy-penitent privilege, the minister's report to the attorney may violate that privilege. Second, the attorney may feel (or be) compelled to report the abuse, especially if the attorney's state has a mandatory reporting statute for attorneys. Ministers who want both to report suspected child abuse, and also to remain anonymous may need to become creative to do both. However, some prudent thought before reporting can lead to possible solutions for achieving both goals.

4. Distinguish between learning about an incident of abuse directly from the abuser who confesses, versus someone who knows about the abuser or abuse. Communications that are confessions are protected in many states as privileged communications. However, these can be learned only from abusers themselves, not from a secondary source. Ministers should remain aware as to who tells them about an alleged incident, so as to know all the facts accurately, and then determine what to do, based on those facts.

5. Determine whether there is "reasonable cause to believe" that abuse has occurred. Typically, mandatory reporting statutes require that a person report if there is "reasonable cause to believe" that abuse has occurred. This does not usually mean that the minister must investigate the situation. It simply means that a reasonable person in the minister's position should report the abuse if there is a likelihood that the suspicion is true. Ministers who question whether to report should ask themselves whether a reasonable person in such circumstances would similarly feel compelled to report. This test may seem ambiguous, but it is used daily by courts to determine issues of disputed fact.

6. Consider whether to exercise the clergy-penitent privilege, if it is available. Sometimes ministers may strongly desire to immediately report a suspected incident of child abuse. However, in some cases, they may believe it would be best for all parties, including the child, not to report immediately. It is in these instances that ministers must be fully familiar with both the reporting and the clergy-penitent pivilege statutes in their states. In such cases, they should see or review the advice of an attorney on these issues.

7. In the event that ministers must or decide to report an incident of child abuse, they may be asked for specific, relevant information:

a. the name of the child allegedly abused, if known;
b. the child's whereabouts;
c. the name and address of the parents or guardians of the child;
d. the nature and extent of injuries, and evidence of a causal link between the alleged act of abuse and the injuries themselves;
e. any evidence of previous injuries; and
f. the identity of the person allegedly responsible for the abuse.

Usually, ministers are not required to investigate any more facts than they are told or otherwise learn. Their knowledge may not include all the above information, and in most cases, they will not be asked or required to learn more.

8. Care for all parties involved—including the alleged abuser. It is easy for emotions and tempers to flare out of control when reports of child abuse surface. However, ministers must resolve to maintain control and consider the well-being of all parties involved. Certainly special attention must be paid to the most vulnerable parties, the children. But it does no good to become uncontrollably angry toward the abuser, who presumably has a serious problem. Such anger may force abusers to respond with anger and thus further complicate and antagonize the situation. Alternatively, an abuser may flee in the face of anger. In this event, the minister and all others may miss an opportunity to attempt to implement justice, repentance, and healing.

Ministers can become integral parts in resolving cases of child abuse. But they should not presume to become the reporter, prosecutor, judge, jury, enforcement agency, and social worker. All professionals who work with child abuse exist so that an entire network of people can attend to the complicated facts that almost always swirl around these cases. Ministers should responsibly report suspected cases, then work with other professionals in the system to bring closure and healing to the situation.

Confidentiality and Privileged Communications

Ministers should consider the following measures in order to comply with and take full advantage of the clergy-penitent privileged communication laws in their state:

1. Maintain high standards of confidentiality. Don't speak openly, in public places, about personal aspects of people's lives. Keep personal records, letters, and documents about parishioners in safe, private places, where others cannot readily see or obtain them. Talk frequently (at least four times a year) to staff members, to remind them that the entire church's reputation rides on the ability of the staff to maintain dignity and confidentiality for its parishioners.

2. Clarify the limitations of confidentiality early in counseling. Most confidentiality problems arise in the pastoral counseling setting. Ministers may be told something which they then decide should be referred to another professional more qualified to handle the problem. If counselees know a minister's policy on confidentiality and referral from the outset, it will save all parties much grief and misunderstanding, if questions regarding this issue later arise. If a minister's jurisdiction requires clergy to report child or elderly abuse, the counselees should be apprised of this in writing at the first counseling session. If the church maintains a policy of referring suicidal or homicidal threats to others more able to help with such situations, again, the counselees should have this in writing prior to delving into the actual counseling.

3. Err on the side of confidentiality rather than disclosure. Attorneys frequently say to one another, "Be loyal to your clients. But don't go to jail for them by refusing to tell a court the client's confidential communications when the court demands to know them." Arguably, the same rule of thumb does not apply to ministers. Roman Catholic canonical law considers it a "crime" for a confessor to betray a penitent.[26] Many Protestant churches similarly promote the highest views of confidentiality.

The goal in maintaining such views of confidentiality is to encourage open and honest communications between parishioners and clergy. Confessing sins not only has a cathartic affect for the person confessing, it also can bring healing as ministers offer guidance and referral to those who come for help.

Ministers should certainly obey the law in their state. But in many instances, the mandatory disclosure law is not always clear, and ministers will need to rely on prayer, wisdom, and experience to determine whether and what to report. Ministers should almost always initially assert the privilege to attorneys and courts that demand to know personal information about parishioners. This will demonstrate the minister's high view of confidentiality and preempt later claims by a parishioner that the minister did nothing to protect a parishioner's privacy. When ministers are confronted with an ambiguous area and are genuinely convinced that they should remain silent for the welfare of a parishioner, they should seek the advice of an attorney and, in the meantime, remain silent.

4. Develop written confidentiality policies. Many denominations and churches have begun to develop their own policy and procedure manuals on confidentiality, for counseling and for the general life and ministry of the church. Such manuals are an excellent way to maintain high standards of confidentiality. These written policies also give direction and a defense that the church did its best, if ever faced with legal issues resulting from dealing with suicidal counselees, cases of incest, child abuse, or the like. Such manuals should be concerned not only with ordained ministers maintaining confidentiality, but also with lay youth leaders, pastoral assistants, secretaries, and other staff members maintaining the same degree of integrity.

The only danger of churches having written policies on these matters is that many courts will then closely scrutinize whether church personnel followed their own rules. If a church or its staff and board draft written policies and procedures, the church staff must follow those guidelines to the letter.

5. If you must reveal confidential information, attempt to obtain a waiver. Any minister may, at some time, decide to discuss or report a parishioner's personal problem. As noted, often the information that needs to be reported is learned in counseling.

Ministers who must report such information about someone will have greater peace of mind if the person about whom they report has signed a waiver of consent for the minister to discuss the information with another appropriate party.

Ministers may obtain such waivers by asking a counselee for the waiver just prior to reporting. A better way, however, is to use the initial counseling session as an opportunity not only to show a counselee a written statement of the church's policy on confidentiality, but to have the person also sign an agreement acknowledging that he or she has read and understands the policy and consents that the minister may report or discuss the counselee's case with other appropriate parties, if necessary.

Some may argue that such a waiver establishes an initial rapport of suspicion, rather than trust, in the counseling relationship. However, many ministers and licensed counselors commonly have counselees sign such releases at the beginning of counseling. They present them as an agreement of honesty and care between the minister and parishioner/counselee. The counselee agrees to commit to all necessary counseling sessions and to be completely open with the minister. The minister agrees to do everything possible to aid the counselee in fully healing any malady from which he or she may suffer.

CHILD PORNOGRAPHY

In addition to other areas of child abuse, recent laws have made it easier for state and federal prosecutors to pursue those who solicit, obtain, possess, or disseminate pornography, particularly when it involves children. Ministers who respond to pornographic advertisements, often unsolicited through the mail or internet computer services, run a great risk of discovery, prosecution, and ultimate public ruin. Federal laws have been enacted to prevent the sexual exploitation of children through pornography distributed by mail.[27]

Recently, these have been amended to include child pornography received, distributed, or otherwise shipped through computers as well.[28] Violators of these laws are liable for up to ten to fifteen years imprisonment and hundreds of thousands of dollars in fines.

Some courts have interpreted these statutes liberally, to convict a person who *knows* of child pornography being delivered to the home, even if the defendant did not personally order it, but it was ordered by another person living in the home. Such courts reason that even though the defendant did not actually order or personally receive the pornography, the defendant knew it was being delivered to their house.[29]

While courts and legislatures are still wrestling with how to regulate pornography on the Internet, they probably will not have any more tolerance for those who knowingly receive and send child pornography through computer or wire services than for those who send it via U.S. Mail. Ministers who ignore biblical mandates of personal purity should bear in mind that dabbling in any pornography, even in one's home, may carry heavy and ultimately humiliating civil and criminal penalties they had not anticipated.

The reality is that every year, most ministers probably learn of at least a few suspected incidents of child, elderly, or some other kind of abuse. Not all such cases are reported. Each instance is delicate and must be dealt with on a case by case basis. Some of these cases are only vaguely suspected, while others are probable or absolutely known. Each case involves a different degree or kind of abuse and requires different treatment.

In recent decades, our society has seen a rise in the awareness of child and elder abuse, and abuse of the mentally ill. Evidence shows that it is not only far more prevalent than many presumed, but also that the tentacles of damage caused by such acts are more far-reaching than many expected. Churches certainly have a right to maintain the confidentiality of the lives of their parishioners. But that right is not an absolute entitlement. It must be balanced against society's very legitimate interest in learning about the existence of child or elder abuse. Efforts to cleanse our society of abuse will necessarily involve those of many groups, including ministers, teachers, social workers, police personnel, foster parents, and the medical and legal communities.

No single group can presume to solve the problems resulting from such abuse alone. In working with others in society to prevent and stop the abuse of children, ministers will act as beacons of care, help, and compassion for some of our society's most vulnerable individuals.

CHAPTER 4

Sexual Misconduct

Shun fornication! Every sin that a person commits is outside the body; but the fornicator sins against the body itself.

I CORINTHIANS 6:18

*I*n the early part of this century, it was not uncommon for legislatures and courts to regulate the sexual and marital practices of the American public. In many countries this is still the case. American laws against seduction and alienation of spousal affections prevented third parties from seducing a married person away from his or her spouse. Beginning in the 1920s and 1930s, however, numerous states began to repeal and abolish laws against these amatory actions. Legal moves away from regulating the public's sexual practices is the result of American society's increasing preoccupation with personal choice, the decriminalization of many sexual activities, and a growing skepticism about whether the law should enforce personal morality.[1]

Despite the reduction in governmental monitoring and regulation of the general public's sexual behavior, the last ten to twenty years have shown an increase in the legal regulation of the sexual conduct of ministers. This appears to be due to two developing aspects of the ministry profession. First, clergy, particularly in the counseling context, have great influence over their parishioner counselees. Because ministers are spiritual and congregational leaders, parishioners place great trust and respect in them, often sharing intimate and delicate details of their lives. For this reason, the clergy and parishioner/counselee relationship becomes a special relationship of trust, considered by some courts to be a "fiduciary relationship." Many have argued that this particular fiduciary relationship, like all the others, should be regulated by law. In the same way that ministers stand to do enormous good for the parishioner/counselee, they also have the potential to do great harm, if they are negligent or intentionally choose to violate the vulnerable counselee in some respect.

Second, more clergy and their churches have begun to offer, and even advertise, counseling services which increasingly resemble professional counseling. As a result, many courts and legislatures believe that the clergy should be regulated in the same way licensed therapists are regulated. Because of these two aspects of ministry, courts and legislatures have allowed (and in some ways, encouraged) plaintiffs to proceed with certain lawsuits against clergy and their churches for acts of alleged sexual misconduct.

Sexual misconduct is one of the most multifaceted legal violations a minister can commit. It is easier to understand when broken into four areas of law: (1) sexual abuse against children; (2) sexual misconduct against adults; (3) sexual harassment in the workplace; and (4) the liability of a church or denomination because of the misconduct of its employee or minister. This chapter will address areas 2, 3, and 4. Area 1, sexual abuse against children is discussed in chapter 3, on child abuse. In addition, this chapter gives certain defenses available to ministers and their churches when accused of sexual misconduct. Finally, we will look at some preventive and responsive actions that ministers and their churches may take, both before and after sexual misconduct claims have been filed.

CLERGY SEXUAL MISCONDUCT WITH ADULTS

As with child sexual abuse, clergy who commit sexual miscon duct with *adult* parishioners may also face civil and criminal penalties. Recently, commentators have divided existing cases of clergy sexual misconduct with adults into two categories. First are those clergy who carelessly or negligently become involved with their parishioners, often in the context of counseling. Second are "predatory" clergy, who intentionally and actively prey upon the sexual vulnerabilities of their flock. This distinction may be accurate. At present, however, these two types of cases are not treated differently under the law. The most recent and important laws which have impacted clergy who have become sexually involved with their parishioners are examined below.

FACT SCENARIO

The Reverend Anderson was forty-five years old when he moved to New Brighton, a midsize midwestern town, where he assumed pastoral duties at his third parish in eighteen years. By most measures, he had a successful life in ministry. He had been at his first two parishes for nine years each, and was generally well-liked by his parishioners. Still, Reverend Anderson was not particularly satisfied with his ministry or with his life. He had had high aspirations when he initially entered the ministry. He had presumed and hoped that it would be a profession in which he would be loved and, to some degree, idolized. But he often found his tasks menial and administrative, rather than glorious and lofty. He was married and had two children, and while his marriage was going fairly well, it had lost much of its original spark. His children were in their late teens and seldom home.

Not long after Reverend Anderson assumed the pastorate at New Brighton, he began counseling Elizabeth, an attractive twenty-nine-year-old woman with marital problems. Her husband, Dave, traveled in his job and attended Reverend Anderson's church only occasionally. Elizabeth had been married in her early twenties, and she and Dave had not gotten along well most of their married life. Dave was a gruff, hard-nosed business-man, with little patience or time for spiritual interests and endeavors. Elizabeth, on the other hand, was very interested in church and spirituality. She was continually disappointed that Dave did not have the same interests.

In addition to her marital problems, Elizabeth had a history of serious depression, which twice had caused her to seek psychiatric help. During one prior episode, her psychiatrist had prescribed an antidepressant to help her through the most difficult period.

Initially, Anderson met with Elizabeth once a week, but soon they agreed to increase their appointments to twice a week. Elizabeth greatly appreciated the counseling sessions because Anderson was interested in and truly concerned about her problems. Reverend Anderson also appreciated the sessions because

Elizabeth made him feel wanted and interesting, at a time when others in his life did not.

At the end of one evening session after about two and a half months of counseling, Elizabeth hugged Reverend Anderson and told him he meant a great deal to her. He reciprocated the hug and said that he had appreciated getting to know her, as well. Each of the next couple of counseling sessions also ended with hugs, which continued to increase in duration. After the third or fourth time, Elizabeth kissed Reverend Anderson on the cheek, telling him that he was the kindest man she had ever met.

Despite the positive effect that Elizabeth claimed the counseling was having on her, she had a counseling session with her previous psychiatrist and told him that her depression was deepening. The psychiatrist again prescribed an antidepressant, believing that Elizabeth was entering a deep clinical depression. Elizabeth told all this to Reverend Anderson. Over the next few counseling sessions, Anderson and Elizabeth continued to hug and had begun to kiss after the sessions. Then it was not long until they had sexual intercourse, first at Reverend Anderson's office, and thereafter, a few times at a motel outside of town.

Two months after they had begun to engage in sexual intercourse, Elizabeth determined that she no longer had any interest in remaining with her husband. She confronted Dave one evening, telling him that she was having an affair with Anderson and that she wanted a divorce. Dave responded explosively, but not with physical violence toward Elizabeth. He immediately telephoned Reverend Anderson, calling him obscene names and telling him that he had violated both his and Elizabeth's confidences. Anderson was unable to respond before Dave slammed down the telephone.

Elizabeth did not see Reverend Anderson again for counseling. Instead, Dave agreed to go with Elizabeth to a licensed marriage and family therapist whom they both knew and trusted. Over a two-month period, Dave and Elizabeth were able to reconcile many of their differences. Elizabeth agreed that it had been wrong for her to become involved with Anderson. During further counseling sessions with the new therapist, Elizabeth became angry because Reverend Anderson had involved himself sexually with her.

She became convinced that he had taken advantage of her weak mental and emotional state during their counseling sessions. Finally, Elizabeth filed a lawsuit against Anderson for sexual misconduct, alleging a variety of legal theories, including breach of fiduciary duty, clergy malpractice, and intentional infliction of emotional distress. Elizabeth's lawyer also told Reverend Anderson that further claims might be made against him based on certain new state statutes, if it were determined that the statutes were in effect at the time of his sexual misconduct with Elizabeth.

Civil Liability

In the above scenario, it is Elizabeth, not her husband, who is suing Reverend Anderson. Lawsuits filed by angry spouses, such as criminal conversation, seduction, or alienation of spousal affections, have been abolished in most jurisdictions, based on the changing social policies of personal and sexual relationships. Courts and legislatures have grown increasingly reluctant to regulate adult situations which appear to have been, at least in some ways, consensual. Also, courts have questioned the prudence of a paternalistic government which tries to protect the feelings or personal morality of individuals. Currently, in most states a lawsuit such as the one outlined above would be more likely to succeed if brought by Elizabeth.[2]

The Reverend Anderson has wisely hired an attorney to defend him. While numerous causes of action were alleged by Elizabeth, all her theories are based upon certain legal principles which an increasing number of courts probably would affirm under similar circumstances. In essence, Elizabeth rightly argues that Anderson, in his role as a clergy/counselor, took advantage of her weak psychological condition.

Reverend Anderson may want to argue that the relationship was consensual. After all, he did not hold a gun to Elizabeth's head to get her into his counseling office in the first place. And she initiated the hugging and kissing. Thus, he did nothing that Elizabeth didn't agree to do. Additionally, he may also argue that he is a human being, like anyone else. And he was not the picture of mental and emotional health either. He was having a midlife crisis of his own, in which he felt unappreciated, overworked, and unfulfilled in his church work. His own marriage was suffering from a lack of excitement, and he had lost enthusiasm for his vocation.

Numerous courts, however, still might reject these arguments and find in favor of Elizabeth, for a number of reasons. First, some courts may find that because Anderson was her pastor and engaged in counseling with Elizabeth, there was a disproportionate distribution of power, in which he had the advantage. He had the ability to woo Elizabeth into his counseling office by publicly advertising his ministerial counseling services. That he charged no fee only made his counseling services *more* tempting to prospective counselees. He held himself out to Elizabeth as one who could help her with her emotional problems. He represented himself as trustworthy—the least likely person to abuse a counselee in any way.

Elizabeth had come to Reverend Anderson for counseling in a weakened emotional and mental state. Because of his position as a minister and counselor, Elizabeth divulged the most intimate details of her life and placed absolute trust in him. After having divulged, she became extremely vulnerable and developed a strong emotional dependence upon him as a counselor. Then Reverend Anderson engaged in sexual activity with her.

While some courts might have sympathy for Anderson's situation, an increasing number would not. Some courts may find that he had developed a fiduciary relationship with Elizabeth, or a relationship wherein he was in a unique position to help, as well as to harm her emotionally, mentally, spiritually, or physically. It would not matter that he did not intentionally prey upon Elizabeth or have any intention of injuring her. Many courts still might consider his behavior reckless. The power imbalance between him and Elizabeth is enough to make him liable for resulting injury or damages that Elizabeth could prove in court.

Some attorneys might even argue that Reverend Anderson's role as a clergyman increases his power over counselees, because he is viewed as having a more direct link to God and unique powers of absolution. There have been suggestions that clergy sexual abuse is worse than sexual abuse by a secular counselor, because the damage takes on cosmic proportions. Often the victims are shunned by other church members, so they leave the church, losing both their pastor and their community of faith. Some victims sexually abused by clergy may even believe that their relationship with God has, in some ways, been violated, because they have lost any trust in the sacred. While such arguments may sound too theological or lofty for a courtroom, attorneys still may argue these theories in representing sexually abused parishioner-counselees.[3]

Finally, Elizabeth's attorney claimed that he might raise certain statutory causes of action against Reverend Anderson, if the state statutes to which he referred were in effect at the time of Anderson's violations. Some states, including Minnesota and Wisconsin, have enacted or are presently proposing to enact statutes that would impose civil liability upon clergy for sexual exploitation of their parishioners. Under these statutes, any person who suffers injuries caused by sexual contact with a religious counselor has a civil cause of action for recovery of all resulting damages.[4] Under such statutes, *consent on the part of the victim is often not a defense.* Instead, the plaintiff only needs to establish: (1) that a religious leader was counseling the plaintiff for some mental, emotional, or spiritual problem; (2) that the minister engaged in some form of intentional sexual contact with the plaintiff; and (3) that the sexual contact damaged the plaintiff. Under these circumstances, as long as Elizabeth could establish the three elements of the statute, she would have a successful suit against Reverend Anderson, holding him liable for his sexual acts with her.

Criminal Liability

Radical as it sounds to many clergy, some states have adopted, or propose to adopt, statutes which criminally sanction clergy who engage in sexual behavior with counselee/parishioners. Intended as a deterrent to such acts by ministers, these laws may include penalties from fines and probation to mandatory counseling for the clergy, and even imprisonment.[5] If such a statute were in effect in Reverend Anderson's state at the time of his sexual acts with Elizabeth, he might be found guilty and sentenced accordingly.

Defenses to Elizabeth's Civil Claims

Reverend Anderson's attorney probably would raise several defenses against Elizabeth's civil lawsuit, with varying degrees of success. Elizabeth has sued Reverend Anderson on the three legal theories of clergy malpractice, breach of fiduciary duty, and intentional infliction of emotional distress. Sometimes church members suing a minister under similar circumstances may also allege battery or "outrageous conduct" (often synonymous with intentional infliction of emotional distress), but Elizabeth's claims are fairly typical.

First, Anderson's lawyer could argue that the clergy malpractice claim should be dismissed, because to date no jurisdiction has allowed a successful claim for clergy malpractice.[6] This has been a successful defense in many cases—especially when the facts involve some type of negligence in counseling. Nevertheless, such a defense may not get Reverend Anderson far in this case, because some judges have recognized the possibility of successful clergy malpractice claims.[7] The court might allow the plaintiff to proceed with her clergy malpractice claim in this case, because it involves circumstances of an affirmative act of alleged *sexual* misconduct, rather than negligence in counseling.[8] Even if clergy malpractice or alienation of affections claims are dismissed, the court still might allow the plaintiff to succeed on other legal theories, such as breach of fiduciary duty, invasion of privacy, or intentional infliction of emotional distress.[9]

Clergy malpractice is an important cause of action that has created much litigation against pastors, and this will be discussed at length in chapter 5. As it pertains to the above scenario, however, it is worth noting that even if Reverend Anderson successfully defended himself against the clergy malpractice claim, he would still incur costly attorney's fees to defend that claim or to have it dismissed.

Anderson may have a more difficult time raising effective defenses against the breach of fiduciary claim. High courts in some states have held that a minister who intentionally engages in sexual activities with a counselee, and somehow causes injury to that person, may be liable for damages resulting from breach of fiduciary duty.[10] Reverend Anderson's attorney may argue that in a Colorado case called *Destefano v. Grabrian,* although the Colorado Supreme Court ruled that a priest who engaged in sex with an adult parishioner was liable for breach of fiduciary duty as a marriage counselor, that priest was *not* deemed liable in his capacity as a clergy person.

If Elizabeth sued Reverend Anderson only in his capacity as a clergy person, such a defense could defeat her breach of fiduciary duty claim, as well. This defense would most likely succeed in those states where the state legislature has exempted clergy from prohibitions against sexual intimacies between mental health professionals, therapists, psychologists or psychiatrists, and their patients or clients. However, it is equally conceivable that many courts might find the argument of Reverend Anderson's attorneys artificial and an attempt to skirt the real issue before the court. After all, Anderson had sex with a parishioner/counselee over whom he exerted great emotional, mental, and spiritual influence. Clergy who engage in sexual relations with counselee/parishioners, and then are sued, should not presume that courts will exonerate them based upon distinctions between their roles as ministers and their roles as marital counselors.

What about Elizabeth's claim for intentional infliction of emotional distress? Reverend Anderson may want to argue that he is not liable for any damages from this claim,because he did not *intend* to upset or injure Elizabeth. However, for a personal injury lawsuit to succeed, a plaintiff need not prove that the defendant had an evil motive. The plaintiff merely must prove that the defendant intended to do a particular act that resulted in damage to the plaintiff. Thus, even if Reverend Anderson were morally innocent, that is irrelevant to Elizabeth's legal claim. That he intended to have sex with her while she was his counselee is sufficient to prove the intent element of this cause of action.

Elizabeth also would need to prove that the conduct was *outrageous*. Conduct often is deemed *outrageous* if it was intended to "shock" the plaintiff, and if it transcends all bounds of decency tolerated by society. Some courts have been reluctant to recognize this legal claim because of the inherent ambiguities in whether a person was really "shocked," and in determining society's boundaries of decency. In the above fact scenario, however, Reverend Anderson knew of Elizabeth's heightened vulnerabilities to emotional injury if she became sexually involved. Also, it may strike many judges or jurors as extreme and outrageous that Anderson engaged in sex with this married counselee who came to him, in the first place, for counseling regarding her failing marriage!

As for the damages element, Reverend Anderson may successfully argue that Elizabeth cannot prove any actual damages, based on her claim of intentional infliction of emotional distress. Because this is a claim usually allowable *without* a showing of any physical injuries, many courts require a stronger showing of actual damages, such as subsequent diagnosable psychiatric or medical problems resulting from the intentional act of the defendant. Nevertheless, if Elizabeth can show that she underwent further and extra therapy with a licensed therapist, or that she was traumatized in ways that had detectable effects because of Anderson's sexual exploitation, she may well succeed in her emotional distress claim.

Finally, Reverend Anderson may attempt to raise a defense based on the First Amendment. It defies the imagination, however, that any court would acknowledge that ministers have a constitutional right, based on their religious beliefs, to sexually exploit their flock. Anderson would almost surely lose this argument.

PREVENTIVE MEASURES

Single ministers must be especially cautious of awkward situations that might result from dating within the church. Married ministers, however, must also be circumspect to avoid scenarios that may even *appear* questionable or put them in compromising situations. Assuming that readers do not intend to commit predatory acts of adultery or fornication with parishioners, the two lists at the end of this chapter, "Preventing and Addressing Acts of Sexual Misconduct in the Church" and "Damage Control After False Accusations of Sexual Misconduct," should be helpful in avoiding and addressing the circumstances that lead to adult sexual misconduct lawsuits against clergy

SEXUAL HARASSMENT CLAIMS

Sexual harassment in the workplace is the third major type of sexual misconduct that often is disputed in courtrooms; ministers and other religious workers are also employers and bosses. As such, they are required to act within the limits of state and federal law regarding employment and fair treatment of workers. Since Clarence Thomas and Anita Hill argued about alleged sexual harassment before a Senate subcommittee, prior to Thomas's appointment to the United States Supreme Court, many states have struggled to more clearly define and sharply enforce state sexual harassment laws. Those efforts have not been easy. As the following fact scenario illustrates, often it is difficult to determine whether an employer's acts are simply socially inappropriate (or even immoral), or whether they are actually against the law.

FACT SCENARIO

Reverend Wade had never worked at a church as large as his most recent senior-pastor appointment. Cynthia Martin, a bright thirty-three-year-old recent seminary graduate, was the coordinator of ministries and right-hand staff member to Reverend Wade. She worked closely with him daily on almost all projects. Reverend Wade was not only Cynthia's boss, he also was on the denominational committee that would oversee the advancement and ultimate approval of Cynthia's ordination.

Reverend Wade appeared to be happily married. Still, he frequently announced to staff members that he thought Cynthia a very attractive person and that he felt very comfortable working with her. During the initial three months of his new appointment, Cynthia said that she enjoyed working with Reverend Wade. At times, however, she also had found him somewhat sexist in his remarks to her and about women in general. But Cynthia was a self-confident and forgiving person. She merely attributed such comments to Wade's cultural background and his long-standing experiences in more rural church settings.

But one day Reverend Wade stepped over Cynthia's boundary of tolerance just prior to the beginning of a Sunday morning service. He and Cynthia were in an office just off the sanctuary, having a few last words about the order of service. Suddenly, Reverend Wade took a step back and looked Cynthia up and down. He then stepped forward, placed his arm loosely around Cynthia's shoulder, and looked her directly in the eyes.

"Cynthia, I am a happily married man. But if I were a single Christian man your age, I'd find you to be one of the prettiest single Christian girls in town, and I'd ask you out so fast it would make your head spin." Cynthia was instantly uncomfortable.

Reverend Wade then shot a quick glance at his wristwatch. "Oh, man," he exclaimed, "we have to get into that service." He flung open the sanctuary door, quickly slipped in, and began to process down the aisle to begin the service, leaving Cynthia standing in the church office, stunned and confused.

A week passed. Not wanting to overreact, Cynthia did not say anything to Reverend Wade about the incident. However, she made a brief notation of it in a work journal and complained about it in a telephone conversation later that week with her mother, who sympathized with her.

The following week, Reverend Wade and Cynthia had to stay late at the church on Saturday in order to finalize plans for a special, elaborate Sunday service the next morning. That night, around 8:00, Reverend Wade asked Cynthia if she would like to conclude the evening by having dessert at a nearby cafe. Cynthia was uncomfortable with the offer, both because of the incident the prior week and because she thought it might look inappropriate if parishioners saw the two out together at a cafe on Saturday night. Still, she felt compelled to go because she was still getting to know Reverend Wade as her boss, and she wanted to make a favorable impression on him, especially because his opinion could affect her advancement toward ordination. So she agreed to go for dessert.

The two arrived at the local cafe at about 8:20 P.M. Reverend Wade dominated the conversation during the half hour they were there with a discussion about the kind of women he had dated and was attracted to prior to his marriage. He emphasized to Cynthia that most of the women he *really* liked looked much like Cynthia. She smiled uncomfortably and said little. Finally she reminded Reverend Wade that they had an early and long day the next day and said she needed to get home. Reverend Wade agreed, wished her a pleasant evening, and the two parted.

Again, Cynthia was left confused as to whether Reverend Wade was making sexual advancements toward her or was again simply being imprudent in his comments, considering their employment relationship.

This time she called some minister friends from other denominations to discuss the two incidents. Her friends had mixed reactions to the incidents. Some said that Wade certainly had been insensitive and presumptuous, but that Cynthia should ignore the gestures as "hickish" and forgive him, because he did not sound mean-spirited or overtly sexual. Others, however, said that his comments and actions, no matter how sincere, constituted sexual harassment, and he should be confronted. Cynthia again decided to take no formal action.

Two weeks passed after the dessert incident. Reverend Wade and Cynthia were busy with many matters and had little contact. Then one Monday afternoon, Reverend Wade and Cynthia were working alone together at the church. Other staff members had either stepped out or were engaged in other projects. Reverend Wade and Cynthia had begun discussing what she would need to do in order to further advance in her ordination process in the denomination.

Suddenly, he gave Cynthia an odd side glance and a smirk, and said, "Cynthia, I know what you could do for me *personally* to advance more quickly in your ordination process." For a minute, there was an uncomfortable and deafening silence. According to Cynthia's later statements about the incident, Reverend Wade appeared to be looking for a reaction. Then, just as suddenly as he had made the comment, Reverend Wade burst into loud and obnoxious laughter.

Cynthia stood speechless in front of him for about 30 seconds. Then Reverend Wade said, "What?" He paused, looking surprised. "I was only kidding!" Another uncomfortable 15 seconds ticked past. "Don't you know that I was just joking? Can't you take a joke?" Reverend Wade insisted.

"That's hardly a joke, and I quit!" Cynthia shouted with a shaking voice. She admitted later that she was still unsure at that time if she should have accused him of sexual harassment. She *was* sure, however, that she had been deeply insulted by the cumulative effect of Reverend Wade's inappropriate and sexually oriented comments and gestures toward her over the last few weeks. Cynthia turned and quickly walked out of the office and out of the church for the rest of the day.

She was furious, bewildered, and upset. This time, she contacted other clergy in her denomination, telling them of her experiences. They all agreed that Reverend Wade's behavior had been highly inappropriate. But, like the other ministers she had consulted, those in her denomination were also divided as to whether his actions and comments actually broke the law and amounted to sexual harassment.

Cynthia decided that she thought Reverend Wade's acts were sexual harassment. She went downtown to file a claim with an agency which oversaw, investigated, and prosecuted employment sexual-harassment claims. She filed a formal complaint against Reverend Wade, based upon the above described events. When Reverend Wade was served with Cynthia's complaint for sexual harassment, he was shocked and angry. He admitted to other church staff members that the incidents were factually true. But he said that his actions were innocent and Cynthia's claims of sexual harassment were groundless. He called an attorney to represent him and proceed with the case through the courts, if necessary.

SEXUAL HARASSMENT LAW

Sexual harassment in the workplace is a matter of state and federal law. States differ in particular aspects of sexual-harassment law, especially in their definitions and enforcement of these laws. However, many states have adopted the principles and definitions (if not the identical text) found in Title VII of the Civil Rights Act of 1964, which prohibits, among other things, sexual discrimination. Religious organizations and their employees generally are subject to the same gender-based discrimination prohibitions as secular organizations.

Sexual harassment is, indeed, not easy to define in our pluralistic society of diverse ideas of what is politically correct. However, under Title VII and many state laws, sexual harassment is defined and interpreted as: (1) unwelcome sexual advances; (2) requests for sexual favors; and (3) other verbal or physical conduct of a sexual nature. Based on these definitions, sexual harassment can occur in many situations, not simply when blatant physical conduct or demands for sexual favors occur.

Sexual harassment often occurs under one of the following circumstances. First, when the conduct of an employer or superior is of a sexual nature and requires an employee, explicitly or implicitly, to submit to that conduct as a term or condition of employment, it may be deemed sexual harassment. In other words, it is as if the employer is saying, "Submit to 'X,' or you're fired."

Second, when submission to or rejection of conduct of a sexual nature by an individual is used as the basis for employment decisions affecting that individual, it may be deemed sexual harassment. The employer is saying, "Submit to or accept 'X,' and you'll be more secure or closer to advancement in your job."

Finally, when conduct of a sexual nature has a purpose or effect of substantially interfering with a person's work performance or creating an intimidating, hostile, or offensive work environment, it also may be considered sexual harassment by courts or administrative agencies reviewing sexual-harassment claims. In this instance, the employer is saying, "Put up with 'X,' or you may choose to leave." Obviously, these practices are increasingly outlawed as sexual harassment, because they strike most of us as a very unfair abuse of power by an employer over an employee.

The above definitions and descriptions reveal that sexual harassment can take a variety of forms, ranging from subtle pressure for sexual activity to overt physical advances. Examples of sexual harassment are often listed in the sexual-harassment policies of many secular companies or law firms. The following list of prohibited conduct is typical, but not exhaustive:

1. Threats or intimidation of sexual relations or sexual conduct that is not freely or mutually agreeable to both parties.
2. Continual or repeated verbal abuses of a sexual nature, including graphic remarks abut a person's body.
3. Sexually suggestive objects or pictures in a work area that may embarrass or offend a person.
4. Sexually degrading words to describe a person.
5. Advances, flirtations, or propositions of a sexual nature.
6. Obscene gestures.
7. Physical touching of a sexual nature.
8. Threats or insinuations that a person's employment, wages, promotional opportunities, job assignments, or other conditions of employment may be adversely affected by not submitting to sexual advances.

Many sexual-harassment infractions are never complained about, because of a variety of practical problems associated with such claims. Most sexual-harassment accusations cannot be decided by general, sweeping rules of law. Instead, they must be decided by a judge, jury, or administrative agency reviewing the specific facts in each case, over many months. The appeals process may drag a case out even longer. People who accuse an employer of sexual harassment usually no longer feel comfortable working at their jobs during a pending sexual harassment lawsuit. Thus, they quit before or at the time of filing the claim, and are forced to look for another job. Even if an aggrieved employee proceeds with a sexual harassment claim, sexual harassment cases often have unpredictable results. These difficulties, plus the embarrassing nature of many such claims, often discourage parties from pursuing their claims against the alleged wrongdoer.

In the scenario described above between Cynthia and Reverend Wade, the minister's words and conduct may be construed by a court as a suggestion that Cynthia's ordination was conditioned upon submitting to Reverend Wade's sexual advances. His acts also may be viewed as having created an intimidating, hostile, or offensive work environment. In either event, Reverend Wade may have violated sexual harassment laws. In a hearing before a court or administrative panel, Cynthia would most likely argue that Reverend Wade's statements of a sexual nature were continual and repeated, since they occurred on three different occasions, and always when the two were alone together. She also could argue that his remarks were sexually suggestive, embarrassing, and offensive to her, even if he intended them merely as distasteful jokes. Cynthia could argue that he had made several advances toward her, as well as at least one explicit proposition of a sexual nature. Cynthia might even raise the claim that he had physically touched her in a sexual way when he touched her shoulder while complimenting her before the church service.

DEFENSES

Several legal defenses that ministers may make to specific claims of sexual misconduct have been discussed earlier in this chapter.

One defense often raised is that the other party "consented" to engage in sexual acts. In cases of child molestation or abuse, such a defense typically is useless because children are deemed legally unable to consent to such acts because of their tender age and innocence. In cases of adult sexual misconduct, however, a consent defense may be effective to defeat some legal theories, such as clergy malpractice or other claims. After all, in many instances of sexual misconduct, the party claiming to have been abused may also have engaged willingly in sexual activities with that minister. As noted above, however, many courts will not focus on whether the minister intended evil toward the alleged victim. Instead, it will focus simply upon whether the minister intended to engage in sexual activities with the person.

If the person claiming damages is a parishioner/counselee and is claiming sexual misconduct damages based upon a breach of fiduciary duty, a claim that the minister did not intend to harm the person probably will not succeed. The court is not focusing, in such claims, upon whether the minister intended harm, but whether the minister intended to act sexually with a parishioner/counselee. In general, clergy should not rely upon claims of lack of intention to elude liability for sexual acts done with their parishioners/counsellees.

PREVENTIVE MEASURES AGAINST SEXUAL HARASSMENT LAWSUITS

The fact scenario described above is not only plausible, but common. Lawyers and state agencies which regulate employment increasingly hear such accusations—not only against secular employers, but also against churches, religious employers, and ministers. Laws regarding sexual harassment continue to develop and have become more widely used in many states. A sexual-harassment accusation by a church staff member, particularly if levied in the form of a formal complaint against a minister, could have devastating effects upon the minister's reputation in the community and congregation. Ministers would do well to remember a few key things in order to avoid sexual-harassment claims being filed against them.

1. **Implement prudent organizational structure.** As heads of staff, ministers should:
   a. insure that policies are adopted and clearly understood that all forms of sexual harassment are prohibited by all staff members; and
   b. insure that a confidential reporting structure is in place for employees to report alleged instances of sexual harassment.

2. **Err on the side of caution.** As a personal matter, ministers should carefully review the above stated definitions of sexual harassment. Although these definitions are not the sexual-harassment laws in every state, they are representative of many, and may be even more stringent than in many states. If clergy conduct themselves according to the above definitions and examples of prohibited acts, they will reduce considerably the likelihood of avoiding the circumstances that lead to sexual-harassment claims.

3. **Think about your circumstances.** Carefully consider the variety of circumstances that may create sexual-harassment claims. Particularly, review the enumerated list above which gives specific examples of how some parties may perceive that they are being sexually harassed.

4. **Don't presume that others know what you are thinking.** Particularly with employees, don't presume that other parties know you are not serious if you make a personal joke or remark about another. Avoid altogether making sexually suggestive remarks or jokes, either verbally or by conduct. Parties cannot, and are not required to, read your mind when it comes to sexual-harassment claims. The standard of review in the vast majority of judicial arenas to determine whether sexual harassment occurred will be whether a "reasonable person," based on a preponderance of the evidence, would have viewed your conduct in a sexually suggestive way, in violation of a state's sexual-harassment law.

   Never in American legal history have employers and employees been required to be so circumspect in their behavior in order not to violate sexual-harassment laws. Because ministers can least afford scandalous claims against them in their communities, they should be particularly cautious in this regard.

5. **Dating on the job?** Dating relationships that develop from work relationships are not *per se* sexual harassment. Indeed, some wonderful relationships have developed from romances between co-employees. However, if relationships between employers and employees, or superiors and subordinates in hierarchical organizations go sour, this may lead to misunderstandings and often results in awkward or even impossible work environments for those involved. Many employers thus discourage dating of employees altogether. At the

least, employers should advise great caution in such circumstances.

6. **Stay apprised of developments in the law.** Periodically, attend seminars and/or read literature on developments in sexual-harassment laws in your state. Because this is a rapidly developing and popular area of the law, news reports about sexual-harassment laws frequently appear in local and national newspapers and on television newscasts. It is worth reading these updates. New developments could very directly affect your large or small church staff.

7. **Live up to your calling.** Many in ministry have wisely redefined their standards of conduct by deciding to be "unreasonably righteous" (without, of course, being self-righteous). They consciously operate with dignified behavior toward all, especially fellow-employees. Reaffirm that First Thessalonians 4:3-7 is more than Paul's pious platitude when he exhorts:

> For this is the will of God, your sanctification: that you abstain from fornication; that each one of you know how to control your own body in holiness and honor, not with lustful passion, like the Gentiles who do not know God; that no one wrong or exploit a brother or sister in this matter, because the Lord is an avenger in all these things, just as we have already told you beforehand and solemnly warned you. For God did not call us to impurity but in holiness.

Ministers who have engaged in or contemplate engaging in sexual misconduct with parishioners should bear in mind the criminal and civil penalties that are available to victims who decide to prosecute clergy who break the law in this way. Clergy should not rely upon their insurance to cover the cost of defending against sexual-misconduct claims or liability for acts of sexual misconduct. Many insurance policies explicitly exclude coverage of sexual-misconduct claims in the policy language.

Finally, acts of sexual misconduct are committed by people, not by denominations or churches. Yet because many ministers don't have large assets, victims usually turn to the denomination or church for recompense from damaging acts by ministers. Denominational and church leaders should consider the following section to avoid incurring liability from sexual misconduct by their churches' ministers and church workers.

THE CHURCH AND SEXUAL MISCONDUCT

The early 1990s revealed an emerging trend of lawsuits against ministers and churches that appears to have increased unabated ever since.[11] No one would reasonably argue that if a religious worker has broken the law, he or she should be able to hide behind the cloth. However, many fear that if media attention merely sensationalizes these suits, emphasizing multimillion dollar settlements and jury verdicts, innocent clergy may become the targets of popular allegations. Not only might the innocent be forced to pay large defense costs associated with unmeritorious suits, but the damage to their reputations that accompanies these lawsuits is often irreparable.

The following discusses three of the most important issues in dealing with both true and false accusations of clergy sexual misconduct:

Church Liability for the Misconduct of Clergy[12]

Although acts of sexual misconduct are committed by people—individuals, not denominations or churches—it is usually the denomination or church that victims turn to for recompense. This is because churches are usually insured or simply have more money than individual ministers.

The judgment and settlement amounts paid by churches for claims resulting from the acts of their clergy are staggering, reaching into the multimillions and possibly even into the billions.[13] No denomination appears to be immune from the increasing claims of sexual abuse by the clergy.

No church can stop these lawsuits from being filed. But churches can minimize the risks of such claims by changing the kinds of circumstances that often lead to such lawsuits. If churches wish to avoid lawsuits for alleged wrongful acts by their clergy, then they should understand the legal theories under which they may be held liable, and the factual circumstances underlying those theories.

Victims generally have sought to hold churches and religious societies liable for the sexual misconduct of their clergy under four main theories: (1) respondeat superior; (2) agency; (3) negligent hiring; and (4) negligent supervision. The following briefly defines each of these legal doctrines.

Respondeat Superior

"Respondeat Superior," or "let the employer answer," means that an employer will be held liable for the acts of its employee, if those acts were within the employee's scope of employment. In the context of churches, most courts have held that, in order for conduct to be within the scope of employment, the conduct must be "in accordance with the principles of the church or in some way in furtherance of the purpose of the church or religious society, or foreseeable or characteristic of the church or religious society."[14] These same courts have determined that sexual misconduct by clergy is not within a minister's scope of employment.

Although it may seem obvious that churches do not employ clergy to abuse parishioners, some courts have *not* defined "scope of employment" so narrowly. Some courts have held that even abuse which arises out of the confidential relationship that exists between ministers and their parishioners *is* within the scope of employment. Indeed, as the number of claims increases, some believe that more courts will subscribe to this broad definition of "scope of employment." Therefore, churches must continually do all they can to limit opportunities for abuse of such confidential relationships.

Agency

Plaintiffs bringing actions under an "Agency" theory are claiming that clergy (the agents), or even board members or trustees, are acting on behalf of the church, and thus binding the church by their words or actions. This theory has generally been rejected by courts where denominations can show that they have no control over the actions of individual churches or clergy in those churches. However, churches must never assume that they will be immune from a successful claim under this theory. Because many churches maintain at least some control over their clergy, denominations should clearly define, in written policy and procedure documents or in correspondence to their clergy, the areas in which the clergy are *not* authorized to act on the denomination's or church's behalf.

Churches should repeatedly make clear that any sexual misconduct by clergy members, whether verbal or physical, is *not* authorized or condoned by the church. If any such conduct is reported, the church should immediately denounce the misconduct, make clear that the minister, if truly guilty of the act, was not acting on behalf of the church, and follow through with any disciplinary procedures provided in their policies.

Negligent Hiring

Plaintiffs also bring claims against churches under the theory of "Negligent Hiring." This issue may arise, for example, when a church hires a person to work with youth, and the worker molests one of the young people. "Negligent Hiring" means that the church did not exercise due care in hiring an offending worker, or the church did not adequately screen the applicant to discover criminal propensities. Although these actions have had only moderate success, allegedly injured parties continue to file lawsuits on this theory. All churches must constantly guard against such claims by establishing procedures and policies that will help them spot and deal with such potential problems before they hire someone that puts them at risk.

Negligent Supervision

Churches can use reasonable care in hiring workers, yet still be liable if the church fails to exercise due care in supervising them, under the theory of "Negligent Supervision." Churches have been sued and deemed negligent for acts ranging from the sexual abuse of minors, to injuries or deaths occurring during church camping or sporting activities. Churches probably will be found liable for negligent supervision if a court determines that the church failed to exercise reasonable care in supervising its employees, thereby creating an unreasonable risk to parishioners. Also, a church may be liable if the church knew or should have known that a clergy member's conduct would subject third parties to an unreasonable risk of harm. Again, written policies and implementation through training could minimize the risk that such claims would succeed.

Preventing and Addressing Sexual Misconduct in the Church

Historically, sexual misconduct by clergy has been taboo—ignored or dealt with in secret. However, the recent deluge of cases against several denominations demonstrates that churches no longer can afford to ignore the current increase in claims. Churches must face this issue head on, for the well being of their parishioners, and for the churches' survival.

The key to avoiding clergy sexual misconduct and the resulting liability is to establish clear policies and procedures that openly and forcefully address the misconduct. Even if some injurious acts still occur, a church may not be liable, if a court later determines that the church took reasonable precautions, through its policies and procedures, to prevent the injury. Churches should consider instituting at least the following policies to avoid incidents of and liability from sexual misconduct by ministers and church workers.

Look under the sheep's clothing.

One way to be more sure of an employee or clergy member is to do a formal background check before making a hiring decision. Background checks should include calling past employers to inquire about history of aberrant behavior. Especially if an applicant is to work with youth, children, or other more venerable groups, churches are urged to telephone state and local police in past geographic residences of an applicant for a criminal background check to identify potential abusers. By making a thorough background check, churches can avoid the claims often later raised by plaintiffs that the church "negligently hired" or "negligently supervised" a church worker.

Education

Churches should make clear statements about their positions on all kinds of sexual misconduct and should openly discuss with both parishioners and clergy the kind of conduct acceptable and *not* acceptable to the church. This provides an opportunity for churches to express their beliefs and concerns with respect to sexual misconduct and to make clear the high level of moral conduct churches expect from their clergy.

In addition, churches should instruct ministers to avoid situations that suggest even a hint of improper conduct. Most sexual misconduct claims against clergy and churches thus far have stemmed from alleged occurrences in the counseling setting. Thus, churches should instruct their clergy to give special attention to the time, manner and place of counseling sessions between clergy and counselee. Red flags of caution should occur to church workers counseling under emotionally charged circumstances, as when dealing with a troubled marriage or suicidal counselee. Ministers should consciously avoid acts or suggestions which could be construed as undue or unfair influence over an emotionally wrought person. Most clergy approach counseling relationships with the best of intentions. But, in the present legal climate ministers cannot be too circumspect when counseling any parishioner.

Balance the interests of all parties.

Once a claim of sexual misconduct against a minister has been made, church members and officials are often at a loss as to what to do. Because the truth of sexual misconduct claims is often not immediately clear, churches must balance and be concerned for the interests of *all* parties—including the alleged victim *and* the alleged abuser—until one party's version is proven true. Churches might consider the policy of setting up the following groups for each party in the event of an allegation and denial of sexual misconduct:

a. Victim Support: The facts from many recent sexual abuse cases reveal that although true victims of clergy sexual misconduct need the support and understanding of their church, they are often ignored, disbelieved, or even held in contempt for accusing the minister. Even if a church is unsure of exactly what occurred, churches would do well to take the complaining party seriously. It could set up a small support group to prevent victims from feeling abandoned. The existence of such a support group will encourage those who have truly been victims of sexual misconduct to report the incident to the church because they will see that the church will not ignore their claims or immediately discount their credibility.

b. Support the Accused: Charges of sexual misconduct can permanently destroy the reputation of any minister. Ministers are not excluded from enjoying the benefits of due process under the United States Constitution. Similarly, religious workers accused of sexual misconduct should not be deprived of those rights under a church's or denomination's constitution. The United States Constitution guarantees that an accused person is innocent until proven guilty. At the same time that churches select a group to support an alleged victim of sexual abuse, the church should also designate another group of individuals to support the accused minister, and to help direct him or her emotionally, legally and spiritually through the ordeal. If the allegations turn out to be false, such groups can aid in preventing the falsely accused from feeling embittered and betrayed. If the accusations are true, the support group may be instrumental in fostering restitution and repentance.

Many denominations and churches have recently asked whether they should institute a policy of temporarily suspending or placing on leave a religious worker accused of sexual misconduct. As a general rule the answer to this question is no. Such a suspension is highly defamatory to the minister's reputation. And although church officials handling these controversies often try to keep them totally confidential, they are often not successful. Also, again, as a matter of fairness ministers are entitled to due process until the accusations are substantiated.

Some exceptions to the above general rule may be instated as a matter of church policy. For example, if the accusation is child molestation or abuse, churches may determine that the damage to the alleged victim or other children that may occur if the accused *is* guilty, outweighs the damage to the minister from a possibly wrongful temporary suspension. Thus, the church may decide to suspend the minister from working with children, although he or she could continue ministering in other capacities. Also, churches may legitimately suspend a minister based upon a sexual misconduct claim, if the immediate evidence reasonably indicates that the accusation is very possibly true. It would, indeed, be irresponsible, for example, for a church to suspend a minister based on mere allegations, even temporarily, if the accused minister had the airtight alibi that he was not even in the country during an alleged incident of sexual misconduct. In order to make a determination of the relative merits of temporary suspension of a minister because of alleged sexual misconduct, the following procedures and safeguards are recommended to church governing bodies:

1. An immediate and confidential preliminary hearing should be convened. Neither accusers nor accused should be required to prove the merits of their claims on a moment's notice. But if a religious worker is to be suspended and formally accused of an act that could ruin his or her life's work and reputation, that person is entitled to an immediate and confidential opportunity to respond to the accusations, so that a disciplinary body can determine the relative merit of the claims prior to the suspension. This hearing is preliminary to a full-blown trial on the merits of the complainant's claims.

2. Probable cause should be determined. The standard for assessing the merits of a complainant's claims of sexual harassment against a minister at the preliminary hearing should be something akin to the standard used in a police arrest situation. Based upon the alleged facts as presented by all parties, there should exist a reasonable likelihood that the accused minister committed the act. Although the alleged victim should not have to prove his or her allegations with absolute certainty, he or she should have the burden of proving a reasonable likelihood of the truth of the allegations before the minister is suspended.

3. A substantial risk of future harm should be present. A minister's reputation, especially regarding moral issues, is all that he or she has for effective and credible work among a congregation or community. Before the minister is required to take a leave of ministry pending determination of the charges, a disciplinary body should determine that there is a substantial risk of future harm if the minister is *not* suspended. In other words, the disciplinary body should weigh the respective potential injuries to the alleged victim if the allegations *are* true, versus the damage to the minister if he or she is suspended from doing ministry.

Because children are more vulnerable to abuse and influence, there may be an inherent greater likelihood of substantial risk of future harm in cases of alleged child molestation or abuse. In cases of alleged sexual misconduct with adults, absent accusations of rape or forced sexual advances, arguably the likelihood lessens, because no law may have been broken if it turns out that the accused and the accuser were consenting adults.

In determining the risk of future injury, disciplinary bodies considering the evidence at preliminary hearings should take into consideration factors such as (a) the nature and severity of the alleged misconduct; (b) the frequency of the acts; (c) the age, vulnerability, or competence of the alleged victims; (d) any history of misconduct on the part of the accused religious worker, and whether that history involved the same or similar kinds of acts as the present allegations. This list is not exhaustive.

It is a serious matter to commit sexual misconduct. But it is also a serious matter to accuse and suspend a minister or religious worker of reprehensible acts which represent the opposite of what they stand and labor for.

Encourage clergy and parishioners to report to objective third parties outside the local church.

When accusations have been made, churches should encourage clergy members and accusing parishioners to avoid face-to-face confrontations. Because of the highly charged nature of the controversy, such confrontations often become ugly. Parties should consider reporting any accusations or defenses to church leaders outside of the local parish. Any attempt by clergy members to approach their accusers alone may be viewed as an attempt to cover up misconduct or use the position of trust to coerce a retraction. In addition, such confrontations can create situations where other types of misconduct, such as rage or even violence can occur, even (or perhaps especially) if the original claim was false.

Deal with reports quickly.

Churches must deal with reports of abuse immediately. If the accusation is true, this will help churches avoid liability by quickly disaffirming any "agency" relationship with respect to the misconduct. More importantly, immediate action may protect truly abused parishioners from further abuse, and will offer swift vindication to the victim.

If the accusation is false, rapid reporting and collection of information will more likely defend innocent clergy members from false accusations, before evidence is disposed of and memories fade.

Document investigations.

Churches should carefully document investigations into allegations of sexual misconduct. The evidence gathered during such an investigation can be essential also in the guilt or innocence of an accused. Either way, documentation is a critical element and should be meticulously handled by churches investigating allegations of sexual misconduct. Also, a well-documented investigation may help protect denominations and churches from claims of wrongful termination, if they are forced to fire or dismiss a minister for misconduct.

Conversely, they may aid churches in supporting and protecting clergy who have been falsely accused. If lawyers are retained to conduct the investigation, much of their material also may be privileged and protected from discovery by the attorney-client privilege and/or attorney work product doctrine.

"Every appearance . . . ."

Finally, in all situations, remember the apostle Paul's admonition to "test everything; hold fast what is good. Abstain from every appearance of evil" (I Thess. 5:21-22).

Damage Control After False Accusations

The thought of being falsely accused of sexual misconduct makes most of us a little queasy, especially when it is we who are accused. How does one best respond to such an accusation? If you get angry, people will accuse you of being defensive. If you remain calm, they will say you are suspiciously underreacting. And since most of us react irrationally, unpredictably, and often imprudently, propelled only by rushes of adrenaline when such accusations threaten our livelihoods, advice like, "just be yourself," is usually unhelpful and shallow. So what is the best way to respond to such false claims?

An article appeared in the *Wall Street Journal* on how employers in the secular workplace should best respond if falsely accused of sexual harassment.[15] Many of the observations and directives from professional career advisors and consultants quoted in the article are also applicable and valuable advice for clergy wrongly accused of any kind of sexual misconduct. The following highlights some of the suggestions from that article that are especially applicable to church workers:

Don't retreat into hopeless despair.

Your job and your reputation *can* survive even a crisis of this magnitude. (Remember, many in the church may be on your side, even *before* you offer an explanation or response.)

Keep a cool head.

Angry outbursts diminish your leadership authority and may give you accuser more credibility. "Rage," notes one eminent career strategist, "is too often associated with guilt."[16]

Instead of anger, remain dignified.

You will better retain your dignity and the respect of others if you restrict your emotional displays to astonishment, hurt, and grief.

Don't take it lightly.

Whatever your response, don't ignore or scoff at unfounded charges of sexual misconduct. Take the accusations as serious. They are.

Avoid face-to-face confrontations with your accuser.

A fatherly pat on the shoulder in an attempt to make peace may give your accuser an opportunity to yell, "Get your hands off me!" Such situations often distort the true intentions of the party trying to make amends. Nothing you say will make a lying accuser change his or her mind now.

Respond immediately.

Report false accusations to a superior immediately, no matter how seemingly insignificant. Preempting a public report of a false accusation against you will bolster your credibility, and let the world know that you want the true facts out in the open from the beginning. Don't wait for a formal complaint to be filed.

Document as much as possible.

When you report to your superior, take as much documentation as you can quickly compile regarding your accuser. Try to reconstruct all relevant meetings or contacts with your accuser. (This is another good reason for ministers to document *all* important events in their ministry, as a matter of course.)

Calm yourself before responding.

As soon as you are accused, take a short time alone or with a trusted friend to collect your thoughts and emotions. Then respond quickly to the charges in the above prescribed ways.

The present intensity of sexual misconduct claims against clergy undoubtedly will pass, but probably not before it gets worse. A church's best defense against true accusations of sexual misconduct is to attempt to prevent the acts from occurring by proactively avoiding circumstances that often precipitate the wrongdoing—and the resulting lawsuits. Similarly, false accusations can be dealt with more quickly and effectively if ministers anticipate how they should respond *before* being falsely accused.

CHAPTER 5

Clergy Malpractice

Again Jesus said, "Simon son of John, do you truly love me?"
He answered, "Yes, Lord, you know that I love you."
Jesus said, "Take care of my sheep."

JOHN 21:16 NIV

*M*any ministers falsely believe that "clergy malpractice" lawsuits are filed only against ministers for alleged instances of sexual misconduct. Sometimes this is true. But many of the earliest and most widely reported clergy malpractice cases were brought by parties claiming that ministers had injured them by exercising *negligent counseling practices.*[1] The clergy, the plaintiffs claimed, had acted below the standards of acceptable care of other similarly situated ministers.[2] The most notable clergy malpractice case, known as *Nally v. Grace Community Church of the Valley,* addressed the legal question of whether ministers, who were considered nonlicensed therapists, had a legal duty to inform licensed therapists (psychiatrists, psychologists, or the like) of a parishioner/counselee's stated intention to commit suicide.[3] The same question could be asked if the counselee might threaten to harm property, or injure or kill another person.

In *Nally,* as in many cases, the claim of "clergy malpractice" was not ultimately successful. In fact, no court, thus far, has allowed a plaintiff to succeed on this legal theory. Ministers, however, should not rest so easily on this information. The language of some courts indicates that under certain circumstances, a successful claim for clergy malpractice is conceivable and still possible.[4] And even though plaintiffs have not yet won a clergy malpractice case, clergy still have had to defend against those claims, often all the way to the supreme courts of many states. The defense costs alone for many of these lawsuits has run into the tens of thousands of dollars, and often produces years of emotional and mental anguish for the ministerial defendants. Thus, despite the apparent lack of success of this claim, ministers should be aware of the kinds of circumstances that lead to clergy malpractice claims, and should avoid those circumstances.

FACT SCENARIO

Bill, a minister, had been counseling a young woman, Jane, whom he knew had a history of serious mental illness, which included recent hospitalization and a suicide attempt. Jane had entered a counseling relationship with the minister under the express condition that he not discuss her problems or anything she divulged to him with anyone else. Bill, who maintains a high view of confidentiality, agreed.

After four counseling sessions, Jane telephoned Bill to say that she was contemplating another suicide attempt. After talking for over an hour, Jane ended the conversation without any improvement in her mood. Bill was in a dilemma. Should he seek emergency help? If he did, would he violate the trust of the counseling relationship? But if he did not, and the woman succeeded at another suicide attempt, what would be the consequence to Bill? Could the woman's parents, for instance, who had expressed antagonism toward religion, somehow hold the pastor responsible for not notifying someone?

Fortunately for Bill, Jane did not attempt suicide at that time, although since that time, she has been repeatedly hospitalized for depression. As many ministers can attest, scenarios like Bill's are not uncommon. In certain similar situations, families of suicide or abuse victims have sued ministers who counseled their loved ones, claiming that the suicide occurred because the ministers acted below acceptable standards of care. Although no court has, as yet, decided in favor of a plaintiff in a clergy malpractice lawsuit, some judicial opinions have ominously indicated that under certain circumstances, a clergy person may be held liable for malpractice, if the plaintiff/counselee can prove that the negligent conduct of the minister injured the counselee. Situations such as the one Bill experienced with Jane have led many clergy and religious workers to ask at least these three questions:

1. What exactly is "clergy malpractice"?
2. What is the likelihood that plaintiffs will succeed in such suits in the future?
3. How can I avoid becoming a defendant in such a suit?

CLERGY MALPRACTICE LAW

What *is* clergy malpractice, and under what circumstances could a minister be held legally liable for this claim? "Clergy malpractice" claims are professional malpractice claims against a clergyperson. Malpractice is a *tort* (i.e., a personal injury) lawsuit, alleging a specialized form of negligence,or *legal carelessness*. The focus of malpractice and negligence claims is whether a defendant's conduct was extraordinarily careless; whether a defendant's actions presented an unreasonable risk to others, to the extent that the defendant should have known to act more carefully in order to avoid injuring the plaintiff.

Specific legal elements are inherent in all malpractice actions:

1. One must be a member of a profession or trade.

2. The professional must have a legally imposed duty to those whom he or she serves.

3. The professional must breach that duty by acting or practicing below a level of competence (or standard of care) normally possessed by members of that profession or trade.

4. The breach of that duty must have caused some injury to another.

Thus, a clergy malpractice action arises when a clergy person owes a legal duty of care to a counselee, the minister breaches that duty by acting below the required level of competence possessed by other members of the clergy, and the counselee suffers injury as a result.

The courts seem to agree that ordinarily, clergy malpractice claims arise from situations that involve pastoral counseling or spiritual guidance. However, applying the above criteria to the clergy in the same manner as other professionals—doctors, accountants, lawyers, and so on—has proved highly controversial. First, although courts generally recognize clergy as members of a profession, some courts may not consider clergy "professionals," in terms of their legal liability for counseling activities. Moreover, the imposition on all clergy of a legal duty and a unified standard of care is even more difficult for courts. Finally, some courts have disallowed malpractice claims against clergy, based on defenses under the First Amendment of the United States Constitution.

The Pros and Cons of Allowing Clergy Malpractice Actions to Succeed

Legal experts are divided on whether clergy malpractice actions should succeed. Advocates for clergy malpractice actions cite many advantages of allowing such lawsuits against ministers.[5] First, clergy should be restrained because of their unique positions to entice the public into counseling. Ministers typically do not charge counseling fees. Often, they already know their counselees or their families, and they frequently make home visitations. Counseling from a minister does not have the social stigma associated with seeing a psychiatrist or psychologist. Indeed, statistics demonstrate that people turn to the clergy first in times of emotional stress.[6]

Those favoring clergy malpractice actions also argue that allowing such lawsuits to succeed offers several positive benefits. The level of minimum competence in clergy counseling would be raised. The public would have greater confidence in the ability of ministers to deal with serious emotional and mental problems. Finally, ministers would be clearer as to what their duties to the public are in counseling situations.

Those not in favor of successful clergy malpractice actions also cite numerous arguments.[7] First, most states already have exempted clergy from licensing requirements, to avoid excessive entanglements with religion, in violation of the First Amendment. Second, many courts have reasoned that even if courts did impose legal duties on clergy within the counseling setting, it would be nearly impossible to fashion a uniform standard of care that would be applicable to all clergy from America's diverse denominational and religious spectrum. Also, imposing legal duties on clergy counselors would cause a chilling effect between ministers and their parishioner/counselees, discouraging truly open communication.

Many have argued that it is unfair to impose legal duties on clergy for negligent counseling, because in religious counseling, it is not always even clear *when* a counseling relationship exists. Clergy counseling may occur in a variety of settings, ranging from informal telephone conversations or classroom discussions, to formal sessions in the confessional or the privacy of a minister's office. Finally, it would be unconstitutional for courts or legislatures to impose techniques from modern psychology upon many clergy, particularly ministers whose theology does not agree with modern psychological practices.

Thus far, those arguments disfavoring successful clergy malpractice lawsuits have won the day. However, as the next section illustrates, this may not always be the case.

The Likelihood of Success of a Clergy Malpractice Claim

What is the likelihood of success of a clergy malpractice claim in the future? Although the answer to this question is unclear, certain indications suggest that a successful action may not be long in coming.

One indicator appears in the notable *Nally* case. In *Nally*, a 24-year-old man, Kenneth Nally, committed suicide after receiving counseling at *Grace Community Church of the Valley* in Southern California, where the Reverend John McCarther was the senior minister. That same year, Kenneth's parents sued the church in a wrongful death action, alleging that their son's suicide was the result of the alleged failure of McCarther and other church counselors to refer Kenneth, whom the staff knew was suicidal, to a licensed professional such as a psychiatrist or psychologist.

The trial court in *Nally* dismissed the case, holding that non-licensed therapists like clergy do not have a duty to refer suicidal counselees to licensed therapists. Prior to the California Supreme Court's final decision, the California Court of Appeals reversed a lower court's decision and held that ministers *do have* a duty to refer suicidal counselees to licensed therapists.[8] That court further noted that the imposition of a negligence standard upon clergy in the counseling setting to prevent suicides, does not violate the free exercise of religion guaranteed by the First Amendment. Many would and do strongly disagree with this. This holding by the California Court of Appeals, however, clearly reveals that some judges are willing and ready to impose malpractice standards and liability upon clergy.

The Supreme Court of California ultimately held that California would not impose a duty upon nonlicensed therapists, such as clergy, to refer a suicidal counselee to a licensed counselor. However, that court also planted a legal land mine for clergy in a brief footnote. It expressly left open the possibility that nonlicensed therapists like ministers, who hold themselves out as licensed professional therapists, could be held liable for injuries resulting from negligence in clergy counseling.

What does it mean to "hold oneself out as a licensed professional"? One of the Justices of the California Supreme Court, Justice Kaufman, stated in a separate concurring opinion that the church counselors at Grace Church *did* have a duty to refer, because they *had* "held themselves out as professionals," when they represented to the public in widely disseminated church literature that they were equipped to handle suicide and other serious mental problems. Kaufman's opinion cited certain evidence:

> [A] church publication entitled, "Guide for Biblical Counselors" (Guide) [asserted that] . . . absent gross psychological causes, such as a brain tumor, "every emotional problem" was within the competence of the pastoral counselor to handle. Among the symptoms or disorders the Guide listed as falling within the pastoral counselor's domain were "drug abuse, alcoholism, phobias, deep depression, suicide, mania, nervous breakdowns, manic-depressive [disorders], and schizophrenia."[9]

It is not hard to see why Justice Kaufman concluded that the Grace Church ministers held themselves out as professionals. Some churches, including Grace Church, may sincerely believe, as a religious matter, that their lay leaders and ministers are able to counsel the most serious mental and emotional disorders. If they believe that, they should take out insurance that covers those pastoral counselors, and be prepared to face the consequences of possibly incurring the same liability as professional licensed counselors.

Another indicator of a possible successful clergy malpractice claim is that lawyers continue to bring such causes of action into courts around the nation. Since *Nally*, numerous other state courts have wrestled with the validity of the clergy malpractice remedy. The Utah Court of Appeals, citing *Nally*, declined to establish a cause of action for clergy malpractice that would impose a duty on a Mormon bishop to make further inquiries into family conflicts alleged by a minor, and then, if beyond his expertise, refer the minor to others who are qualified to treat such problems *(White v. Blackburn*, 1990). The Colorado Supreme Court rejected the remedy of clergy malpractice, finding it unconstitutional *(Destefano v. Grabrian*, 1988). The Ohio Supreme Court refused to find clergy malpractice where a plaintiff alleged intentional misconduct on the part of a minister *(Strock v. Pressnell*, 1988).

However, a dissenting opinion in *Strock* noted that malpractice is a viable action against clergy who are negligent in counseling. But that judge stated that "clergy malpractice" is a misnomer, because the standards for such actions are the same for both secular and religious counselors in the marriage counseling context. Finally, one justice of the Alabama Supreme Court indicated that clergy malpractice may be a viable remedy in that state, although that court declined to find such malpractice where a plaintiff alleged intentional, but not negligent, misconduct *(Handley v. Richards*, 1988).

Some of these opinions reveal that the present lack of success of plaintiffs' clergy malpractice suits does not mean that the possibility of a successful clergy malpractice claim is foreclosed. Instead, the courts are merely awaiting a sufficient egregious factual scenario, before they allow a clergy malpractice action to succeed.

A final indication of the possible success of such an action is that some courts have shown a greater willingness to hold "nontherapist counselors"—the category in which the California Supreme Court has placed clergy—to a higher standard of care than the public at large. For example, the California Court of Appeals, in *Richard H. v. Larry D.*, ruled that a marriage counselor may be liable for "negligent infliction of emotional distress for having sexual relations with a patient's spouse while the couple was receiving marital counseling."[10] Thus, at least in California, it appears that clergy may be held to the same higher standard of care toward marriage counselees as secular marriage counselors are held.

Many clergy wrongly presume that they have blanket immunity from lawsuits under the United States Constitution. Courts have demonstrated that they are not afraid to hold clergy or their churches liable for personal injury claims, if a wrong has been committed. The First Amendment of the United States Constitution does not create blanket immunity for everything clergy do, irrespective of the injury or negligence involved. Numerous courts have held clergy liable for claims ranging from religious fraud to defamation. Although the United States Supreme Court held, in *United States v. Ballard,* that the courts may not challenge the accuracy of one's sincere religious beliefs, it is certainly conceivable that clergy could act negligently in a counseling situation, where their religious beliefs are not challenged.

All the indicators outlined above seem to suggest that future malpractice actions against clergy are likely. Given the high cost and emotional strain of defending such suits, the prudent course of action for clergypersons is to act as if such legal actions already have been successful, and take appropriate steps to prevent problems.

PREVENTIVE MEASURES

The protest from clergy, church officials, and religious organizations against allowing clergy malpractice claims has been overwhelming. In *Nally,* advisory briefs from churches, synagogues, and religious groups around the nation were filed in support of the defendants. One petition included the names of 6,669 churches and related organizations.[11] The lack of success of clergy malpractice claims may have lessened the frequency with which they have been filed in recent years. Still, clergy malpractice claims are not likely to simply disappear.

Since prevention appears to be the best remedy for such claims, it is important for ministers to determine what measures would best immunize them from liability. To do this they should consider the elements of a cause of action for malpractice:

- the existence of a professional relationship which imposes a duty of care upon the professional toward the client (parishioner-counselee);
- identifiable standards to which the professional should be held;
- injury resulting from breach of the duty of care; and
- how existing cases, particularly *Nally,* have addressed the elements of cause.

Presume that you owe a legal duty to the counselee.

Clergy would best protect themselves from liability by presuming the existence of a professional and legal duty to counselees. While case law and commentators may continue to argue that no such duty should exist, a presumption that a duty does exist will keep pastors alerted to the need to maintain high professional and ethical standards in all counseling situations.

Consciously develop high standards in your counseling practice.

The second element of malpractice suggests that clergy should define what constitutes "responsible" conduct in their counseling activities and abide by that level of responsibility. Consciously determining the behavior that is most appropriate for a minister will improve the quality of counseling and simultaneously help reduce the risk of legal liability. Where should clergy turn to determine what might be considered "responsible" conduct for a counselor?

In *Nally,* before the trial judge dismissed the case, plaintiffs' attorney offered expert testimony, which he argued established identifiable standards of care for clergy in the counseling context. Three ministers, who also practiced psychiatry or psychology and were from both liberal and conservative denominations, testified that the following standards were interdenominationally used among responsible clergy:

(1) Investigation—the cleric investigates whether the counselee is serious about suicide (or other potentially harmful conduct done by or to the counselee).

(2) Referral—if no psychologist or psychiatrist is connected with the counseling, and if warranted, based on the investigation, an appropriate referral should be made.

(3) Consultation—vital information should be shared with professionals and nonprofessionals who are in a position to help.

Despite the dismissal of the *Nally* claim, the expert testimony those witnesses offered is instructive for clergy because it suggests some tangible and sensible directives which can be applied in a church's counseling ministries and may help to insulate a pastor from legal liability. Clergy who frequently counsel parishioners should develop a network of responsible professionals in related fields, with whom they can consult and to whom they can refer counselees. That network may include psychiatrists, psychologists, marital and family counselors, and fellow clergy.

Explain your abilities and limitations to counselees from the beginning.

Clergy should also consider what the California Supreme Court suggested in *Nally,* that clergy who "hold themselves out as professionals" may be held to the same high standards of care to which professional counselors (i.e., licensed therapists) are held. Thus, in order to avoid legal liability, all ministers should begin counseling relationships by clearly defining what, as counselors, they are equipped to handle. Clerics should state their limits and inform counselees that if their problems are beyond those limits, appropriate referrals will be made. Although a counselor's disclosure of a counselee's problems to a third party could present problems of breach of confidentiality, counselors will be protected from liability if they clearly apprise the counselees that they will be referred to another professional if necessary.

Make appropriate referrals.

Some ministers may fear that counselees will lose confidence in them if they involve outside professionals, but that criticism is misguided. Patients rarely lose confidence in their general physician when he or she involves a specialist who is better equipped to deal with the patient's specific medical problem. Similarly, if a parishioner trustingly approaches clergy for counseling, the parishioner is not likely to lose confidence in the minister who suggests that the counselee will be better served by a professional more skilled to handle the parishioner's problem. Indeed, a parishioner-counselee may have even greater confidence in a cleric who investigates, refers, and consults, because the counselee realizes that the cleric is in contact with a larger network of mental and physical health workers in the community, all of whom are there to help the counselee.

If you can stand the heat, stay in the kitchen—but beware.

Some clergy may have the training and experience to handle serious emotional problems of members of the community, and they may choose to represent themselves in that manner. Those clergy, however, should be prepared to confront the potential liability of their professional counterparts, such as psychiatrists and psychologists.

Attempt to change the law.

Those interested in limiting the tort liability of clergy might also consider writing to state legislators to encourage them to draft legislation immunizing clergy from malpractice liability. Lawmakers must be educated as to the unique role in society served by pastoral counselors. The *Nally* case may be relied upon in arguing that, for legal purposes, clergy should be considered nontherapist counselors (i.e., nonlicensed), who should *not* be legally bound by state-imposed duties to refer counselees to medical or psychiatric doctors, or other licensed professionals.

Acquire insurance.

Finally, if clergy want more peace of mind against the risk of financial ruin by having to defend against, or being held personally liable for, their counseling actions, they, their churches, and their denominations should purchase insurance which covers negligent acts and misconduct, and specifically includes clergy malpractice. Be sure that the coverage includes the cost of attorneys' fees, as well as the cost of losing a lawsuit. Also, the policy holder should be sure that the policy covers the type of counseling done by the the religious worker. Coverage of $1,000,000 or more is fairly customary.

It is prudent for ministers also to have their own personal liability coverage, in case a conflict of interest between the church and the minister arises. Information on such polices is available through the American Counseling Association, and also through a number of church insurers. Even with such insurance, however, ministers should carefully read the policy to see what types of behavior are not covered.

Throughout the Bible, religious communities have prescribed limits on the behavior of their religious leaders. In ancient Israel, the religious community executed false prophets whose prophecies did not come true (Deut. 13:1-5). Levitical priests were to receive no inheritance from other Israelites, although they were entitled to support by receiving portions of each sacrifice given by worshipers (Deut. 18:1-6). Timothy directed early Christian communities to appoint only bishops, deacons, and elders who met certain social, cultural, and moral requirements (I Tim. 3:1-13; 5:17-22).

Contemporary clergy malpractice actions also attempt to regulate the behavior of ministers. The difference between current actions and the early Jewish and Christian regulations is the source of the regulation. Directives for clergy behavior from within a religious community are, to Americans, probably more palatable than directives for religious leaders prescribed by a state judiciary or legislature.

Unpalatable as state directives may be, odds are that future careless acts by a clergyperson somewhere will force the courts and society to determine the limits and duties of ministers within the counseling context. For example, will society consider it permissible for clergy to discourage parishioner-counselees from taking medications which stabilize their mental and emotional states, if the sole basis for the clergy's advice is an unwarranted self-confidence in the ability to counsel? What if a counselee stops taking some medication and kills himself, or another person? What if the clergy knew that a counselee might commit suicide without the medication, but did not consult anyone else about the counselee's problem?

The scenario that these questions suggest is plausible. If a lawsuit ensues, jurors will judge whether the minister has acted with reasonable care in the circumstances of his or her profession.

CHAPTER 6

Invasion of Privacy

Now there was a Pharisee named Nicodemus, a leader of the Jews. He came to Jesus by night.

JOHN 3:1-2

*M*aintaining the privacy of others goes to the heart of ministry. Ministers are those whom we can trust not to intrude into our personal lives or dealings, until we are ready to share those things with them. They will not be voyeuristic or invade our personal space. We presume that ministers will even avoid listening to gossip about us. And when we are ready to share our private lives with them, we presume that we can confess our darkest secrets without condemnation, reprisals, or publication of those secrets to others. We feel we can confide in clergy, along with our spouses or other loved ones, during times of personal and private difficulties.

For these reasons, if a minister is accused of invading someone's privacy, it is viewed by most as a serious breach of the minister's moral, and sometimes legal, obligation to that person. Such accusations shock our consciences, because we believe that protecting, not exploiting another's privacy, is the very *job* of those in ministry. Allegations that a minister invaded the privacy of another so as to break the law is often devastating to the minister's profession, destroys public confidence in the minister that often took years to establish, and can have long-term negative effects on the spiritual life of a congregation.

In recent years, the legal claim of *invasion of privacy* has gained considerable notoriety. Because of the negative consequences that can result from a minister's indiscretion in these areas, it is imperative that ministers understand and know how to avoid invasion of privacy claims.

Invasion of privacy may result in legal liability from four separate types of conduct: (1) intruding upon another's affairs or seclusion; (2) public disclosure of private facts; (3) false light publications; and (4) wrongful use of another's name or picture.

Because each type may be the basis for a separate legal action, an example of each will be offered, followed by the law regarding it.

FACT SCENARIOS AND CORRESPONDING LAW

The fact scenarios outlined here are extreme situations in which most ministers would *never* find themselves. Nevertheless, they are illustrations of situations that often lead to invasion of privacy claims. Similar but more subtle circumstances certainly do occur, and could ensnare even the most cautious religious workers in invasion of privacy lawsuits.

Intruding Upon Another's Affairs
or Seclusion—Fact Scenario

"It was none of your business and I'm going to sue you!" Teresa yelled as tears streamed down her face in front of the church's board of elders. "You had no right to take my picture in my own home without my consent!"

Pastor Steve, the twenty-nine-year-old associate minister at University Church, sat speechless as Teresa accused him. Steve had photographed Teresa kissing a man other than her husband, Rick, when Rick was away from home on business. Steve took the picture one evening while he was parked in the street outside the home of Rick and Teresa.

Steve claimed that his motivation for taking the photo was legitimate. Rick and Teresa were long-time members of University Church, where Steve had been an associate minister for four years since he had graduated from seminary. Rick and Steve had been friends for many years, even prior to Steve's pastorate at the church. Rick had repeatedly come to Steve in the church counseling office in tears, claiming he was sure that Teresa was having an affair with another man when Rick was gone on frequent business trips. Rick begged Steve to help him find out if it was true.

At first Steve was reluctant to get involved. But, caring for both Rick and Teresa, Steve came to believe that it was his duty and call as a minister to help Rick in his emotional agony and to help save the marriage, especially if Rick's allegations were true. So Steve agreed to take Rick's suggestion that he survey the house with a camera the next time Rick went away. The first time Steve did so, Rick's suspicions were confirmed.

But now, as a result of showing Rick the photograph that Steve had taken, Rick and Teresa were separated, and Rick was insisting on a divorce. Teresa, who now seemed genuinely sorry for her actions, was screaming that Steve had ruined her life, breached his duty to her as a minister, and he would pay for it in court.

The Law of Intrusion into Seclusion

In order to bring an actionable case to court for intrusion into seclusion, a complaining party must prove the following elements:[1]

1. There was *an act of intrusion* upon the affairs or seclusion of the complainant by the defendant.
2. The act of intrusion is *objectionable to a reasonable person* (i.e., to the average person under similar circumstances).
3. That which was intruded upon was truly *private*.

In the above scenario, there was an act of intrusion. Pastor Steve photographed Teresa through her bedroom window. That act probably would be objectionable also to the average person, especially because Teresa was in her bedroom. Finally, the intrusion in this instance was certainly upon something private. Again, she was photographed in her own home and in her bedroom—a place where she should be able to expect privacy.

Pastor Steve may object on a few levels. First, he might claim that it was his religious duty to expose Teresa's wrongdoing. He might even fashion this into a First Amendment defense.[2] This would likely be rejected, however, because, on balance, there are other ways he could have gone about testing Teresa's fidelity to her husband, short of invading her privacy, such as by confronting her. This is not to say that Steve's assertions about his moral and spiritual duties to Rick and Teresa are unimportant. It is simply to say that while those duties are important, they probably would not persuade a court to allow Steve to violate Teresa's rights to privacy.

Next, Steve also might claim that Teresa's bedroom window was not truly private, or he would not have been able to photograph her from the street. Depending upon the exposure of the window to the street, this argument might be more convincing to a court. But it also probably would fail, because if accepted as a defense, nearly anyone could create a defense based upon "lack of privacy," no matter *how* objectionable their acts. Nearly all peeping Toms could claim that the windows they peered through were not private, in some way or other. In this case, Steve's act of photographing Teresa in her own *bedroom* was surely a violation of her privacy.

Finally, Steve might argue that Rick, Teresa's husband, *told* him to photograph Teresa in their home in order to catch her in an act of adultery. Thus, the argument would be that Rick gave Steve permission. Privacy, however, is generally viewed as a personal entitlement. Rick cannot consent for Teresa as to her privacy. It belongs to Teresa. Only she is entitled to give consent to expose her privacy to others. Rick legally could have persuaded Steve, or a private investigator, to photograph Teresa going into a motel with another person. But this is legal because it is a public place. If the intrusion is upon privacy, however, only the person whose privacy is being exposed may consent to the exposure.

Many situations may lead to claims for intrusion upon seclusion, such as instances of eavesdropping, nonconsensual entry into the home of another, or rifling through another's personal records. In intrusion upon seclusion cases, the key focus of the courts seems to be on whether the complaining party had a reasonable expectation of privacy that was objectionably violated. If such was the case, the violator may be liable for damages resulting from the act of intrusion.

Public Disclosure of Private Facts—Fact Scenario

Pastor Edwards printed the following text in *The Chimes*, the monthly church newsletter, in a section called "Pastor's Forum":

I was personally deeply blessed this last week after speaking with one of our newest members about his experience in coming to know Christ. He admits to a long history of drug abuse and sexual promiscuity prior to coming to the Lord and becoming involved here at First Church. While he regrets many personal decisions that he now believes were foolish and destructive, he also now sees God's constant direction in his life, even during his wayward years. We rejoice that he is now with us here at First Church and that he and others like him are willing to share their wisdom and faith with us, as well as their personal trials and failures during years without the Lord.

The newsletter was mailed to the entire congregation of 550 members. The letter was referring to Bob Davis, a new attorney in town and a new member at the church. While the newsletter did not explicitly state that the member to whom Pastor Edwards was referring was Bob, it seemed obvious to all that it was, because Bob had been the only new member to join the church during the last eight months. All three new members who joined in the year prior to Bob were women.

All the things the newsletter stated about Bob were true. What it did not say was that Bob had told Pastor Edwards about his past life in the minister's office, believing that his statements would be kept confidential. Bob was infuriated when he saw the newsletter. Bob, who believes that the statements in the newsletter may damage his reputation, or even his profession, has told Pastor Edwards that he is considering filing a lawsuit for invasion of privacy, based upon his public disclosure of the facts of Bob's private life.

The Law of Public Disclosure of Private Facts

In order to successfully bring a lawsuit for invasion of privacy based upon public disclosure of private facts, a party must prove:[3]

1. There was a publication or *public disclosure.*
2. The publication or disclosure was of *private facts* or information by the defendant about the complaining party.
3. The publicized information was the kind that a *reasonable person of ordinary sensibilities would find objectionable* if made public.

In the above scenario, the publication about Bob was certainly public. It was sent to a 550-member congregation. It was also about private information. It involved issues that Bob even had told Pastor Edwards were now somewhat embarrassing to him. In the pastor's study, Bob had communicated these personal facts to Pastor Edwards as his minister. The publication probably also would be deemed objectionable to the reasonable person of ordinary sensibilities. Although it is common in some churches for parishioners to discuss their past bad acts, in the the context of giving a verbal public testimony of how they came to God, in this case, Pastor Edwards gave Bob's testimony for him. Some may argue that the minister was not overly explicit in his comments about Bob's past life or bad acts, thus the minister did not violate the "objectionable" element in this type of invasion of privacy. Perhaps, but attributing criminal and sexually promiscuous behavior to an adult professional in the community— especially a new adult about whom people are highly impressionable—would be considered highly objectionable by most.

What significance is there that Pastor Edwards did not actually mention Bob's name? If it is determined that it was obvious to a reasonable member of the congregation that the text was about Bob, then Pastor Edwards may not be exonerated on this fact alone. Does it matter that Pastor Edwards actually meant the comments about Bob in a complimentary and kind way? No. To a court, the only issue would be whether Pastor Edwards published private facts about Bob and that the publication would have been highly offensive to a person of reasonable, or average, sensibilities.

It is noteworthy that unlike defamation cases, truth is not a defense in lawsuits of public disclosure of private facts. Bob does not argue that his past life was not scandalous. He simply argues that it should not have been broadcast by the minister in the church newsletter, especially when the minister learned about Bob's life in a private, confidential context.

There is an absolute defense to claims that a defendant wrongfully publicized private facts about another. If the publicized facts are a matter of public record—even if they are embarrassing or scandalous—there is no legal prohibition against publicizing them. Thus, for example, if Bob's past bad acts to which Pastor Edwards was referring had resulted in criminal convictions or divorce, Bob could not successfully sue Pastor Edwards for invasion of privacy. Many published facts, such as criminal records, involvement in lawsuits, ownership of certain property, or bankruptcies, are often embarrassing. Ministers may have moral or biblical reasons for not publicizing such facts. But it does not *legally* invade another's privacy to publish those facts.

False Light Publications—Fact Scenario

Both the Reverend Boyd and Pastor Harris were prominent ministers in the same city, denomination, and ecclesiastical governing body. Reverend Boyd was running for the position of Moderator, the highest office in the denomination. By all estimates, he was far ahead of his challengers.

Pastor Harris was known for fiery, opinionated sermons. Occasionally, however, he was known to make statements with little truth to support them. One Sunday morning during a service with 600 in attendance, Pastor Harris commented on the suitability of Reverend Boyd as Moderator.

Reverend Boyd had been a police officer before entering the ministry. Although he was highly regarded in his denomination, he had resigned from the police force to become a minister at a time when some officers had arrested an unarmed Hispanic man. One of the officers at that arrest had beaten the man so badly that he later died in the intensive-care unit of a hospital. Reverend Boyd had been one of the twelve officers initially present at that arrest. But Boyd had been exonerated in a later civil rights lawsuit filed against the policemen by the Hispanic man's family.

Reverend Boyd had never publicly commented on the incident since becoming a minister. He had, however, stated that the majority of arrests he made as a policeman involved African Americans and Hispanics. But he further stated that he stood by those arrests, believing they were warranted. He said that given a second chance, he would make the same arrests again, regardless of statistics.

Not knowing any more facts than these, Pastor Harris, in his sermon, launched into a strong public criticism of Reverend Boyd as a candidate for the position of Moderator. He referred to Boyd as "an unreflective individual who has willfully participated in a racist arrest. It would be shameful for such a person to represent our denomination as Moderator under any circumstances!"

Pastor Harris's comments were persuasive to his congregation and soon were passed on to other members of other congregations in the denomination. One week after Pastor Harris's sermon, the denomination elected as Moderator a minister *other* than Reverend Boyd. At the next denominational meeting, an informal suggestion was made from the floor that the denomination consider a public censure of Reverend Boyd for his views on race and justice.

Reverend Boyd was furious when he learned of Pastor Harris's comments in his sermon. Boyd considered himself a deeply reflective and sensitive person in regard to racial issues. Although he was one of the police officers present at the notorious arrest of the Hispanic man who had been beaten to death, Boyd had been at the arrest scene only for the first few minutes. Before the Hispanic man was taken into custody, Reverend Boyd was called to another crime in progress. For these reasons, he had been exonerated in the civil rights case.

Although Reverend Boyd has serious misgivings about suing another minister, he believes that a lawsuit for false light publication may be the only effective way to publicly clarify his position and acts regarding race and justice, and to dispel the false light in which he has been placed by Pastor Harris's remarks.

The Law of False Light Publications

If a person gives publicity to another, placing them in a false light, the person may be liable for damages resulting from that publication. To establish a lawsuit for a *false light publication*, a plaintiff must prove:[1]

1. There was a publication about the plaintiff by the defendant which placed the plaintiff in a *false light*. A publication is considered to place a plaintiff in a false light if it attributes:
   a. *views* that he or she does not really hold; or
   b. *actions* that he or she did not take.
2. The false light publication must be *objectionable to a reasonable person* under similar circumstances.
3. The defendant must have publicized the statement with *knowledge that it was false, or with reckless disregard* to its falsity.

In this case, it appears that Pastor Harris's comments indeed placed Reverend Boyd's views and actions regarding race and justice in a false light. First, Harris suggested that Boyd was ignorant, at best, and racist, at worst, in his views regarding minorities. Second, Harris's comments suggested that Reverend Boyd willfully engaged in a serious racist hate crime. These suggestions obviously would be objectionable to reasonable persons, especially if they were ministers, as is Reverend Boyd. Finally, Pastor Harris made his outrageous comments without knowing any of the details of the Hispanic man's arrest, without investigating that arrest, and without acknowledging that whatever the circumstances, Reverend Boyd had been exonerated in the civil rights suit brought against him by the Hispanic man's family.[5]

The third element, requiring that the plaintiff prove that the defendant knew or should have known of the falsity of the publication, is what we described in chapter 2 as "malice." It most typically arises when an issue of public interest exists, or when public figures are involved in a lawsuit.[6] In this case, the facts indicate that Pastor Harris made the statements about Reverend Boyd recklessly, without really knowing the details of the case, and thus this element probably also is met.

Wrongful Use of Another's Name or Picture—Fact Scenario

No one would have thought that little Dave Bossart, who got his start singing in the children's choir at Valley Community Church, would have gone on to become a teen idol and record an album with national sales recognition. But that is exactly what happened. What made it even more remarkable was that Dave was still only sixteen years old.

Reverend Marks thought that Dave's success would be a good means of raising money for the new van needed for the church youth group. Dave Bossart's family had been members of the church for a long time, even though they rarely attended and were not involved in the life of the church. Still, Reverend Marks was sure the Bossarts would not mind if the church used Dave's face on the front of a T-shirt. So the minister had 500 T-shirts made up with Dave's picture on the front and the name of the church on the back. Under Dave's picture, the shirts said, "Dave Bossart got his start at Valley Community Church!"

The shirts were distributed to members, who sold nearly all of them immediately. It was not long before Dave Bossart's mother saw one of the T-shirts. While all the Bossarts had enjoyed Dave's musical success, they were finding it increasingly difficult to handle the fan telephone calls, requests for endorsements, and Dave's unendingly busy schedule that began once his first album was released. The whole Bossart family had grown impatient with everyone trying to get a piece of Dave and his newfound success.

Believing that the T shirts would only add to their family's decreasing personal privacy, Dave's mother called Reverend Marks at the church and asked him to stop the sale of T-shirts. Reverend Marks found Ms. Bossart's attitude snippy. He told her that the T-shirts had already been distributed to be sold. Feeling that Ms. Bossart was ungratefully forgetting all that Valley Community Church had done for Dave's upbringing, Marks unsympathetically added that he thought the church should be permitted to sell the shirts. Ms. Bossart became angry and said that she was going to file a lawsuit for invasion of privacy because of the church's sale of the shirts. Reverend Marks ignored Ms. Bossart's threats and instructed the congregation to sell the remaining T-shirts.

The Law of Wrongful Use of Another's Name or Picture

To successfully sue the church for the wrongful use of Dave's picture, Ms. Bossart need only prove that the defendant church engaged in unauthorized use of Dave's name or likeness for personal or commercial advantage.[7] In the above instance, many courts would say that the church invaded Dave Bossart's privacy by wrongfully appropriating his picture and name for the church's advantage. Some courts limit this legal claim to those who are using another's name or likeness for a commercial advantage. Some such courts may view the above instance as fundraising for a nonprofit cause—the church youth group— and may excuse the church on that basis. Nevertheless, many courts would focus on the fact that Ms. Bossart had made clear to Reverend Marks that the use of Dave's picture and name was unauthorized; thus the church (or Reverend Marks) may well be liable for any damages resulting from the sale of the T-shirts.

Other Considerations for Invasion of Privacy Claims

Certain other factors may come into play if a church or minister is sued for any of the four theories under invasion of privacy.

Causation. The invasion of the plaintiff's private interests must have been actually and foreseeably caused by the allegedly invasive acts of the defendant. If the causative link between the defendant's act and the invasion of privacy were so tenuous that no reasonable person could have foreseen that his or her behavior would offend the plaintiff, then the plaintiff's claim will fail. The reasonability as to whether there was a foreseeable connection between the act of invasion and the damage it may cause is a question for a fact-finder—a judge or jury.

Proof of Damages. In an action for invasion of privacy, a plaintiff typically need only prove the above stated elements under each cause of action. Otherwise, the damages are presumed, based upon the harm to the plaintiff's interest in privacy and the emotional distress and mental anguish caused by the intrusion into the plaintiff's privacy.[8]

Intentional or Negligent Invasion. An invasion of someone's privacy may be intentional or negligent. Thus, if defendants are negligent in some way and invade another's privacy, it will not be a defense in claims of invasion of privacy for defendants to say that they did not *intend* to upset anyone or intrude in an way.

Illegal Tape Recordings. Many states have statutory or judicially decreed laws prohibiting the tape recording of other persons without their consent or knowledge. In some states this is illegal if the communications being recorded are confidential or intended to be private.[9] In other states, it is prohibited simply if the person being recorded has not consented. If ministers do intend to record an otherwise private conversation, they should announce on the tape that the conversation is being recorded, that the parties are aware of it, and that they have consented.[10] A federal statute also exists which prohibits covert tape recordings of conversations without the person's knowledge or consent, where there is proof that the recorder intends to commit a crime or injurious act with the recording.[11]

DEFENSES

In the unpleasant event that a minister is sued for invasion of privacy, a few sure defenses exist to almost all claims.

Consent. If a party consents to allow another to intrude upon otherwise private grounds, then the invaded party loses any later claim to invasion of privacy.[12] Some states require that consent be given in writing. Even where consent clearly has been given, however, if the consent granted is exceeded, then the one exceeding the consent may be liable for invasion of privacy. For instance, if a person grants an interview for a radio news show, and then the interviewer uses the interview and a picture of the person for an advertisement, the interviewer may still be liable for invasion of the person's privacy, because the interviewer has exceeded the scope of the consent given.

Defamation Defenses. The defenses to actions for defamation, based upon absolute and qualified privileges as outlined in chapter 2, are generally applicable to claims for *public disclosure of private facts* and *false light publications*. For instance, a minister may comment, where legally required in a judicial proceeding, on a parishioner's private life.[13] As was noted earlier, however, unlike defamation cases, *truth* is typically *not* a defense to invasion of privacy claims.

PREVENTIVE MEASURES

Maintaining a high respect for privacy is critical to all ministries. Young people, and even children, need a degree of privacy, just as do adults—even though children may not be as likely to file lawsuits if their private affairs are somehow violated. Rather than responding defensively, after someone's privacy has been either morally or legally invaded, all those in ministry would do well to consider observing at least the following protections of privacy.

Don't get personal . . . until you're invited.

Dozens of pastoral scenarios are fertile ground for invading the privacy of parishioners and counselees. Ministers often have knowledge of or access to people's intimate conversations, private actions, personal records, and hospital rooms in ways that few other professionals do. The simplest way you can avoid overstepping your bounds with those to whom you minister is to wait until you are approached, asked, or invited to engage in people's lives at the most personal levels. Before you read letters or view other personal things which you think will be helpful in assisting a person, ask if it is acceptable for you to do so. Walk away from conversations that are not intended for your ears, and of course, maintain as confidential what is unintentionally heard. Knock on hospital room doors and wait for an invitation before entering. Then, once you are invited into a person's personal space, be sure not to enter any farther than you were invited—whether that be emotionally, physically, or spiritually.

Get the owner's permission.

Rights to privacy are personal. Even a spouse typically cannot give up the other's right to privacy. If you are invited into someone's personal realm, be sure the invitation came from the party who actually owns and controls it.

Ask if there is a reasonable expectation of privacy.

Many situations that involve invasion of privacy claims occur relatively innocently. The offending party may have *negligently,* rather than intentionally, invaded another's privacy. Courts usually test whether a place is private by asking whether the person had a *reasonable expectation of privacy* in that place. This is a question for a fact finder, such as a jury or judge, whose instincts usually are much like those of the average person. If a pastor is unsure whether someone's privacy will be invaded, it is best to *err on the side of caution* and wait until either asked or the person can be approached in a less intrusive way.

Keep private facts private.

Even the most confidential ministers find it hard to resist telling a profound story that actually comes from the life of their ministry. Unfortunately, many such stories also come from the very personal lives of parishioners. Most ministers feel safe in relaying stories from the pulpit about previous church experiences. Even this, however, has gotten some ministers into trouble, if they accidentally let slip a name or if the audience, in some other way, knows who the minister is speaking about.

If private facts are told to a minister in the counseling office or on the telephone, or if the minister experiences personal, private moments with parishioners in their homes or in some other way, they would do well to keep those circumstances confidential and not divulge them under any circumstances. Even when it appears to be completely clear that there is no chance of identifying and exposing persons without their consent, use caution. If a story is simply too good to pass up, and the minister feels comfortable, he or she can ask the persons if they mind if the story is told anonymously in a sermon sometime. Assure them that you will keep their identity confidential and respect their privacy.

Get the facts straight.

Even when many ministers have permission or otherwise feel comfortable telling a story about a parishioner, they get the facts so mixed up that they place persons in a false light, sometimes embarrassing them. If you don't know the facts, don't tell the story. Most stories are better told when the facts are fully known, anyway.[14]

Get permission to use a face, name, quote, or recording.

Any public announcement or communication from the church which is designed to raise money and uses a picture, name, quote, or sound or video recording of a person other than the author, should be disseminated with the permission of the person whose likeness is being used or referred to. In some states, the church may need written permission from the referent, and readers should specifically consult an attorney in their state about this issue.

Tell them you are taping.

As noted earlier, state laws vary on the legality of making sound or video recordings of others without their consent. If you are unsure of the laws in your state, you should either wait to consult an attorney or tell people that you are recording or filming. If the person recording is unsure of the laws, and the person being recorded asks that the machine be turned off, it would be wise to do so.

Privacy has been highly prized in ministry since biblical times. The disciples consulted Jesus in private (Matt. 17:19; 24:3; Mark 13:3). Jesus willingly met with covert seekers like Nicodemus, a leader of the Jews interested in Jesus' teachings who came to Jesus in secrecy by night (John 3:1-2; 19:38-40). Jesus prayed with, questioned, and taught his disciples privately (Luke 9:18; Mark 4:34; Luke 10:23). Jesus healed in private (Mark 7:32-35). Jesus encouraged privacy in spiritual life (Matt. 6:5-6, 17-18). Early church leaders conferred privately (Gal. 2:1-2).

The value of privacy in ministry is exceeded only by the damage done when privacy is intruded upon, yanked away from its owner. Privacy is never taken away gently. It is always abrupt, disturbing, and leaves a bad memory. In our day, when so much seems intrusive and tabloid-like and so little remains truly private, precious, and ours alone—to be savored only with those few whom we choose—those in Christian ministry should seek to be the guardians of people's privacy. Of course, damaging secrets such as child abuse must come to light. But other secrets that are ours to treasure should be guarded like gems.

CHAPTER 7

Undue Influence

*Do not mistreat an alien or oppress him, for you were aliens in Egypt.
Do not take advantage of a widow or an orphan. If you do and they cry
out to me, I will certainly hear their cry.*

EXODUS 22:21-23 NIV

Laws against undue influence are ancient, and they are as morally based as they are legal. The Old and New Testament communities had numerous specific directives against undue influence for specific contexts, such as family law, real estate dealings, commerce, employment law, and sexual conduct (see Exod. 22:21-23; Lev. 25:14; 25:17; Deut. 24:14; I Thess. 4:3-6).

Undue influence is a lawsuit for restitution resulting from circumstances in which one person took unfair and illegal advantage of another, thereby exploiting that person. It is often alleged against defendants who also are accused of fraud, but there are at least two major differences.

First, fraud claims focus on the intentional deceit of the actor, whereas undue influence claims focus on the weaknesses or deficiencies of the victim. A person may unduly influence another for illegal gain without misrepresenting any facts. Instead, the actor usually has some superior position over the victim, and typically fails to acknowledge the other's weakness, taking advantage of him for gain. Second, fraud claims are forward looking—they *prohibit* deceitful acts for gain—whereas undue influence is an equitable remedy, to correct damage that has already occurred.

Historically, most American undue influence lawsuits have involved the contesting of wills. However, courts have acknowledged that such lawsuits also are valid in the context of gifts given during a donor's lifetime.[1]

Undue influence lawsuits sometimes are filed against ministers, when someone contests the circumstances under which a minister receives a gift, donation, or bequeath. Ministers often find themselves in positions of superiority, when people seek them out in times of personal weakness—such as when they are ill, elderly, or emotionally or mentally impaired. Ministers are also in positions of superiority over others by virtue of their congregational leadership. Thus, people place extraordinary confidence in ministers, and they often have considerable influence over parishioners.

Because of this influence, when ministers or their churches are given gifts—especially large cash gifts—they may be accused of undue influence, if it appears that they obtained a gift by using their position to gain an unfair advantage over the donor. The test is whether the minister overpowered the will of a giver through undue influence,[2] or whether the gift was obtained through improper means.[3]

FACT SCENARIO

Probably the most stereotypical scenario regarding undue influence lawsuits against clergy is the minister who woos the confidence of a dying, elderly widow. Then when she no longer has all her sensibilities, he persuades her to bequeath her estate to him or to the church. Lawsuits involving such facts have happened all too frequently; suffice it to say that such behavior should be avoided.[4]

In recent years, more public and blatant acts have led to undue influence claims against clergy, and these are the acts that this chapter will address.

The latter part of the twentieth century has witnessed the rise of megachurches. The membership and attendance at these churches is often six thousand or more on Sunday mornings. Such attendance frequently requires these churches to have campuslike facilities, which sometimes include television broadcast stations and seminaries, or other such training centers. Needless to say, such churches usually have annual budgets that rival those of small towns.

In order to fund these ministries, many of the ministers and church leaders engage in elaborate and very public building-fund campaigns, which call heavily on the membership to give as much as they can to spur the greatest growth possible.

Many of these churches have had long and positive ministries, have greatly impacted their communities and the nation for the better, and even have led the worldwide Church in grand new directions. Annual ministers' conferences are frequently offered by such churches, to teach leaders of smaller church how to begin precisely the same ministries in their parishes. The negative side to these ministries, however, is that, too often, they have disputes, in the course of their fundraising, over many aspects of *the way* these funds are collected and used.

In most undue influence cases involving clergy, where it is clear that a minister took at least some advantage of a plaintiff, courts typically wrestle with two competing legal policy issues: (1) When does a moral act of unfair gain by a minister become a legal violation?; and (2) How foolish should the courts allow people to be, before they step in to save them from the results of their decisions to give costly gifts to unscrupulous or overbearing clergy? The answer to each of these questions usually hinges on the specific interactions between the defendant/ministers and the plaintiffs, which led to the gift.

The following fact scenario involves fundraising by a large church. It is based on an actual case decided in the District of Columbia. As with many of the illustrations used in this book, this is an extreme example of the kinds of circumstances that lead to legal allegations against clergy for undue influence Despite the shocking acts alleged in this case, the legal outcome may be even more surprising.

Soliciting Gifts—with a Strong Arm?

The Evangel Temple (the Temple) was a Christian church that had grown in the ten years since it first established its church home in Washington, D.C.[5] The church leadership was comprised of a presbytery of ministers, headed by a bishop. The Temple's property was governed by the presbytery, through a council of elders, ministers, and deacons.

According to the Temple's leadership, it was clear that they needed a new facility for worship and its numerous church activities. On that basis, the pastors and church leadership set out to organize a building-fund campaign for a new facility to be built in a neighboring area. The new facility was to include not only a new church, but also a television facility, a school, a gymnasium, and homes for the church leaders.

There was nothing uncommon about the Temple's stance on giving, published in its by-laws. It read in part:

> We believe that tithing and giving are to be practiced continually by all believers and are an outward expression of the unity of the Church, the Body of Christ, as it joins together in support of the work of the Lord. Gen. 14:20; Lev. 27:30-32; Num. 18:26; Mal. 3:8-10; Matt. 23:23; Rom. 12:8; I Cor. 9:7-14; 16:1-3; Heb. 7:4-10.

The Articles of Incorporation of the Temple further contained a fairly standard covenant requiring that members in good standing offer "willing support of the work and ministry of the church by systematic giving of tithes and offerings, and a conscientious effort to be present in the regular meetings of the church."

Beyond a general agreement, however, about the initial decision to start a building campaign and the church's statements on giving, there was little agreement between the church leaders and numerous church members about what occurred, once the building campaign was underway. Nine church members sued the church and its leadership over the *means* used by the leaders to obtain contributions during the campaign.

The Plaintiff-Parishioners' Claims

The plaintiffs sued the church and its leaders, among other claims, for undue influence. The allegations of all the plaintiffs agreed that the defendant church leaders did certain bad acts which affected all injured parties. Some plaintiffs also made specific allegations, claiming that they were individually injured by acts of the church leaders.

All the plaintiffs claimed that they had been instructed by church leaders that the senior minister, referred to as "Bishop," represented the voice of God. The Bishop had announced that God required each employed parishioner to give $5,000 to the building fund within five months. The deacons, who were the first to be told of this revelation at a retreat, were given thirty minutes to decide whether to give the required amount. The Bishop allegedly threatened that if they did not give, God would curse them, kill them, or "turn his back" on them.

The plaintiffs alleged that parishioners who had not given enough to the building fund were publicly identified and shamed during church services. They were made to walk through a gauntlet between two lines of deacons who had already contributed. The deacons laid hands on them and prayed for them as they walked the gauntlet. Once at the end of the line, if they still failed to pledge the required amounts, they were ordered to leave the church in disgrace.

Some members were threatened with excommunication, and were later dismissed if they did not pay the required sum, or if they questioned the practices of the church leadership.

According to the plaintiffs, the church leaders did not care about the parishioners' ability to pay the required contributions. Those who did not readily have the money were directed to borrow it or sell their personal or real property to obtain the funds to contribute. They were allegedly told to borrow the funds no matter what the interest rate, and to apply to numerous lending institutions for multiple loans. They were allegedly instructed by the church leadership not to tell the banks about the other loans for which they had applied. One couple was publicly praised by the Bishop for obtaining six different loans on the same day, worth $20,000.

Despite the fact that most in the congregation were of modest means, the Temple case reported that many members rose to the occasion and gave relatively large amounts to the campaign. The Douglas family, a couple and their son, gave $24,000. Another couple, the Harrisons, obtained a second mortgage on their home to raise $7,900 to contribute. This reportedly required them to struggle financially to pay an additional $298 a month on their mortgage. One parishioner, who did not have any other source from which to give, contributed child support checks in her $2,000 gift. Another parishioner, who gave over $10,000, went into such financial distress that he had to begin working 100 hours a week. Ms. Moreno, whose annual salary was only $10,000, stated in a deposition that she felt so "brainwashed" and pressured by the defendants that she gave her entire paycheck for a two-week period to meet her $5,000 pledge.

Finally, many of the plaintiffs claimed that the church leaders had misappropriated and diverted church funds for their personal use.

The Church Leaders' Defense

The defendant church leaders, among whom were the Bishop and two of his sons, responded to the claims with an entirely different account of the events. The record reflected that the Bishop testified in a deposition that those who contributed "came gladly, joyfully, and said yes, it is God's will for me to give $5,000, $10,000, $20,000, and $30,000, and $50,000 and $100,000." One of the Bishop's sons testified that he didn't believe that the church leadership had manipulated anyone. The church leaders, according to him, were merely fulfilling their responsibility of "giv[ing] direction to what [they] believed."

The Legal Outcome

The Evangel Temple case never went to trial. Instead, with apparent reluctance and sympathy for the plaintiffs, the trial court dismissed their undue influence claims against the church leaders, stating, among other reasons, that this cause of action had been applied only in the context of *wills* in that jurisdiction. The trial court further found that the plaintiffs had failed to prove by clear and convincing evidence that the defendants had misappropriated or diverted any funds, or had made any false representations of fact upon which the plaintiffs had reasonably relied in contributing their money. Finally, the trial judge concluded that any of the defendants' threats of punishment from God were protected by the First Amendment.

The plaintiffs appealed the case. The appellate court upheld nearly all aspects of the trial court's opinion. The appelate court disagreed with the trial court, however, that undue influence claims are applicable only to wills. Nevertheless, the only part of the lower court's ruling that actually was reversed was the undue influence claim of two of the plaintiffs—Mr. and Mrs. Harrison—who claimed that the Bishop had come to their home personally to solicit funds for the building campaign. However, even the Harrisons' undue influence claim was later dismissed, when the church leaders successfully reargued that the Harrisons had not asserted in their complaint that it was *because* of statements made by the Bishop at his personal visit, that the Harrisons contributed funds to the Temple's building campaign.[6]

THE LAW OF UNDUE INFLUENCE

Why were the plaintiffs' claims against the church leaders in the Evangel Temple case dismissed? To many, this seems patently unjust. Some might also argue that the Evangel Temple case is not really about undue influence at all, since the court dismissed that claim against the defendants. To understand the decisions in this case, one must understand the factors that must be present for most courts to make a finding of undue influence.

First, although this case was ultimately not successful for the plaintiffs, they presented enough evidence for the court to refuse to grant the defendants' request for sanctions, based on their claim that the plaintiffs had brought a frivolous undue influence lawsuit against them. According to the court, while the plaintiffs' claim for undue influence was not winnable, based on the record, there was also sufficient evidence that it was *not* frivolous.

Second, the opinion of the appellate court made clear that, if the facts were truly as the plaintiffs presented them, then virtually all aspects of undue influence *were* present for most of the plaintiffs, except one, to succeed on that claim. There was no evidence of the existence of "confidential relationships" with each of the plaintiffs.

Undue influence is any improper or wrongful persuasion whereby the will of a person is overpowered, and that person is induced to act or not act in a way that he or she would not, if left to act freely. Courts will be more persuaded that undue influence occurred in lawsuits over disputed gifts, if they find that certain factors, or *indicia*, existed in the circumstances surrounding the claim. One of the foremost factors is the existence of a "confidential relationship." (Other such *indicia* include disproportionate gifts made under unusual circumstances, or the age and health of a donor.)

It generally is easier to establish undue influence when a confidential relationship exists between parties, because one party has placed enormous trust in the other.[7] A confidential relationship can mean a *fiduciary relationship*, a legal relationship of trust, where one party is required to take special care to look out for the well-being of another. Also, a confidential relationship can be based upon informal relationships, where one person simply relies upon or trusts another.[8] The appellate court in the Evangel Temple case recognized that these confidential relationships extend not just to legal relationships, but also to moral, social, and personal relationships.

Numerous courts have acknowledged that such informal confidential relationships of trust often exist (although not always) between clergy and parishioners; especially in the context of gift-giving to the church or minister.[9] This is true because parishioners, who are potential donors, often have a psychological dependence on the minister, who then invites them to give. The principal factor in a court finding a confidential relationship between a minister and a donor is the existence of continual contacts, usually on a one-on-one basis, between a spiritual leader and a trusting or otherwise deferential parishioner.[10] Courts scrutinize such relationships more closely, so as to discourage abuse of the trust that creates them.[11]

In the Evangel Temple case, the court decided against the plaintiffs, because the court found that none of them, except the Harrisons, had been solicited one-on-one by the Bishop or other church leaders. The Douglas family who gave $24,000, the woman who gave up her child-support checks, and even Ms. Moreno, who said she had been brainwashed to give up an entire two-week paycheck—all these parishioners had donated money based on directives given from the *pulpit*. The court sympathized with the plaintiffs morally. It strongly inferred that the plaintiffs should be able to trust their ministers, believing that they have the congregation's best interests at heart. But in the end, the court held that there was no evidence of record regarding undue influence, because the plaintiffs had not been *individually* swindled or cajoled into contributing.

Is it good legal policy for courts to allow apparently unscrupulous ministers to solicit such vast amounts from their pulpits, from people who can't afford to give such sums? Arguably, yes. Otherwise, a floodgate of litigation could open from all who claimed that they were unduly influenced by a minister's sermon in some way. The results could lead to endless judicial scrutiny over the contents of ministers' sermons—one of the things that the First Amendment is designed to avoid. Ministers would be required to second-guess everything they preached, wondering if someone might construe their words in the wrong way.

Note that this rule does not apply to *fraud* from the pulpit. If a minister misrepresents, for instance, the financial status of the church from the pulpit, in an attempt to induce parishioners to purchase bonds for a building program, this would almost certainly be actionable. This is especially true if the parishioners relied upon the false statements, invested their money, and lost it because the church failed financially.

But the issue at hand is undue influence in the context of church giving. Despite the moral wrong that these situations reveal, our courts cannot be expected to financially bail out every parishioner who foolishly donates large sums to churches that pressure them for money. Instead, our courts generally take the view that they will allow the public to be, at times, *very* foolish, before the judiciary will step in to challenge the religious rights of churches to solicit funds, or demand that they disgorge donations given by their parishioners.

A Related Claim—Breach of Fiduciary Duty

Claims for breach of fiduciary duty often accompany lawsuits for undue influence, especially if there is a legally recognized fiduciary relationship between the plaintiff and the defendant. Ministers may be deemed by courts to have a fiduciary relationship with some of their parishioners, especially those whom they counsel, or over whom they hold a superior position of knowledge or emotional and psychological influence. In such circumstances, parishioners often place special trust or confidence in the minister, thus creating a legal relationship, wherein the minister (or the one trusted) becomes the fiduciary. As such, under the law, the minister is viewed as having a special duty of care and loyalty to look out for the best interests of the other person.

Clergy do not have a fiduciary relationship under the law with all parishioners simply because they are parishioners. But if they presume that they have such a relationship with those whom they counsel, or from whom they solicit funds or obtain gifts, this presumption will alert the minister to maintain high standards of care during such activities. This is especially true if the potential donors are elderly, ill, mentally or emotionally unstable, or minors.

DEFENSES

The Evangel Temple case demonstrates that there are numerous defenses available to ministers accused of undue influence in soliciting gifts. Of course, this is not to encourage readers to engage in the alleged fundraising tactics of the Evangel Temple. It is, however, to assure ministers who are wrongly accused of undue influence when fundraising or soliciting gifts for the church, that they have an arsenal of defenses available in such cases.

First, ministers wrongly accused of undue influence may argue that no *indicia* of undue influence existed, if such is the case. If there was no confidential relationship, if the donor was in a healthy state of mind and body, and if the gift was only a small portion of the donor's total wealth, these facts will go a long way in convincing a court that the gift in question was not obtained through undue influence. The essence of this argument is that the gift was made knowingly and willingly, and thus was legally obtained.

Ministers also may argue that their fundraising efforts are protected by the First Amendment. Where churches can meet the low threshold of demonstrating that they have solicited funds from their members based on a sincerely held religious belief, courts will be more reluctant to question their acts.

Finally, ministers may defend their position by arguing that the plaintiff failed to prove a causative link between the alleged acts of undue influence and the plaintiff's ultimate decision to contribute. In the Evangel Temple case, the Harrisons' claim for undue influence was eventually dismissed, because even though the Bishop visited them in their home and suggested that they give to the building fund, they admitted on the court record that his visit angered them more than it cajoled them to give. Only later, after attendance at more church services, did the Harrisons decide to give to the building fund.

PREVENTIVE MEASURES

The following preventive measures include many of the same points suggested in chapter 1, "Fraud," because of the similarities between fraud and undue influence. Again, the main difference is that fraud uses *deceit* as its chief tool, whereas undue influence uses unfair advantage over another's lesser or weakened physical, mental, or emotional condition.

1. Does a fiduciary relationship exist? If a fiduciary relationship exists between a minister and another party, wherein the minister has an advantageous position over that party in some way, there will be a heightened scrutiny of the acts of the minister. In all dealings where a minister is relating to a sick person, a child, an elderly person, an emotionally distraught person, or the like, the minister should act with circumspect care, disclosing all facts that the other party may want to know about a proposed gift or transaction.

2. Consider the health of parishioners. If a person's health in any way impinges upon his or her ability to understand a transaction or a gift, that transaction or gift may be more vulnerable to later attacks of claims of undue influence or breach of fiduciary duty.

3. Be attentive to the age of the persons with whom you deal. As in fraud cases, if the plaintiff is older and lacks the sensibilities or awareness of a younger person, or if the plaintiff is particularly young and is naive or unable to understand the gravity of a situation, a court is more likely to determine that undue influence could be the basis of a gift.

4. Don't accept gifts made under unusual circumstances. Gifts made to a minister or church under circumstances wherein the donor was particularly vulnerable to the suggestions of clergy—for example, by a person who is dying or very ill—are more susceptible to later claims of undue influence. Ministers should avoid soliciting gifts under such circumstances. If a parishioner asks that a minister be present while he or she is dying and wants to make a gift under such circumstances, the minister should be sure that others are present at such a meeting. Gifts that represent most or all of a donor's holdings will be more suspect of undue influence than those that represent only a small portion of those holdings.

5. Encourage all parties to seek independent and disinterested advice. Again as with fraud, ministers who encourage the people with whom they deal to seek independent advice, including friends, family members, and attorneys, will help to dispel the appearance of unfair dealings.

6. Be sure that all parties exercise "free will." The essence of undue influence claims is that there was improper or wrongful persuasion, whereby the will of a person was overpowered and that person was induced to act or not act in a way that he or she would not have done if left to act freely. For this reason, parties must be left to act freely and deliberately in choosing to enter into the any business negotiations, transactions, contracts, gifts, or bequeaths. Any conduct used to overpower or unduly influence another may be viewed as undue influence, fraud, duress, or another related claim.

7. Look to the *indicia of honesty* discussed under the "preventive measures" section of chapter 1, Fraud. Just as many of these applied to prevent fraud claims, they also may be applicable for averting claims for undue influence.

8. Create *indicia of care*. Just as we suggested to create *indicia* of honesty in order to counteract fraud, a church can create a policy of *indicia of care* to counteract undue influence issues.

The above warnings regarding undue influence are not exhaustive. Church and religious workers can creatively consider other ways to take added precautions when soliciting gifts or funds for ministry. For example, ministers who approach elderly parishioners for church gifts—especially if they are in nursing homes or seriously ailing—may choose, as a matter of course, to ask one of the donor's family members to be present when speaking to the potential donor. Or the church may decide never to accept gifts that represent more than a certain percentage of a parishioner's total assets. Such considerations could be made part of the church's policy statement and will create a milieu of concern for the well-being of the church's parishioners, over and above the concern for raising money.

First Peter 5:1-3 gives the following directive for church leaders:

> To the elders among you, I appeal as a fellow elder . . . . Be shepherds of God's flock that is under your care . . . as God wants you to be; not greedy for money, but eager to serve; not lording it over those entrusted to you, but being examples to the flock.
>
> I Pet 5:1, 2*a*, 2*c*-3 NIV

According to these verses, the essence of being a pastor is caring servanthood. The parishioners of any church should be able to presume that their pastor has their best interests at heart, when they are asked to contribute their lives and funds to the church. Conversely, the essence of undue influence is self-serving exploitation. Few legal claims could be more antithetical to true Christian ministry.

It would be naive to presume that churches can function without asking for commitments, financial and otherwise, from parishioners. Indeed, numerous biblical references demonstrate that it was common in the Old and New Testaments for church leaders to ask for time, money, effort, and other commitments from their parishioners.[12] Thus, even in encouraging and asking members for true commitment, ministers become obedient to the Scriptures. But both the moral and legal principles require that all be done, not for personal gain, but for the nurture and edification of the Body of Christ.

Responding to Lawsuits

*Going to trial with a lawyer who considers your whole lifestyle a Crime in
Progress is not a happy prospect.[1]*

*HUNTER S. THOMPSON,
U. S. JOURNALIST*

*M*inisters need to respond to lawsuits in two ways—prac-
ically and philosophically (or theologically). As with
anyone who is sued, they must respond practically to
avoid losing a case and having a judgment entered against them
in court. As ministers, they need to respond philosophically, or
theologically, because inherent in ministry is the need to understand, interpret, and explain to the rest of society the meaning
of significant societal shifts, particularly as they affect the church.
This chapter first describes the nuts and bolts of the way ministers
should respond legally, if they, their churches, or their religious
organizations are sued. Second, it offers some sociotheological
explanations as to why Americans are suing their ministers, and
how ministers might best respond.

WHO YOU GONNA CALL? . . .

Being served with a lawsuit is like having a bee land on your
arm, about to sting you. Most of us swat violently at the bee,
flapping our arms wildly in an attempt to get rid of it. Unfortunately, we usually end up hitting ourselves, angering the bee, and
driving its now-penetrating stinger even farther into our skin. A
light shake of the arm, however, would leave most bees unagi-
tated, to fly away on their own without stinging us.

When most people are sued, they panic and want immediately to get rid of the lawsuit. They wring their hands, nervously ranting and raving about the injustice of being sued. They then call a number of people familiar with some of the facts in their case, in an attempt to win them to their side and be assured that they did nothing wrong. Eventually, they call the only attorney they know, usually either a relative fresh out of law school, or an expert in an obscure area of law vastly different from their legal problem.

They quickly tell that attorney an incomplete and garbled version of the facts that supposedly underlie the lawsuit, pay an exorbitant retainer, and later are told that they need to retain a different lawyer who is more familiar with the type of legal problem they are experiencing. Finally, their new attorney informs them that they should not have shredded all those file documents, and they will not be able to call as witnesses those they have telephoned, because their testimony is now tainted by the post-lawsuit discussions.

Even those who do everything this book directs them to do to avoid lawsuits, still may be sued. If this happens, knowing how to respond is critical. This chapter outlines how to respond to a lawsuit without losing your mind, your case, or your money because of acting imprudently or hiring the wrong lawyer.

How *Not* to Respond to a Lawsuit

Ministers who are sued usually feel that they have even more reason to panic than the average defendant. They are, after all, public figures whose moral reputations rest on their credibility. How can they possibly *continue* to minister to a church under the weight of pending legal accusations?

The reality is that in some instances, clergy cannot continue ministry once they have been sued. It becomes even more difficult when the lawsuit against them involves both moral as well as legal claims. If the lawsuit involves accusations of sexual misconduct—especially involving children—ministry becomes almost impossible. It is often wisest to step down temporarily, or the church could allow the defendant to continue, but only after the defendant offers an immediate demonstration of probable innocence at a formal preliminary hearing, prior to a complete trial on the facts. Ministers should *not* do any of the following:

Don't Ignore the Lawsuit.

Typically, defendants have twenty to thirty days to formally respond to most lawsuits. If they fail to respond, their silence is construed by courts as an admission of guilt. If they continue to ignore the suit, a judgment may be entered against them in the amount asked for in the complaint.

Ministers, in particular, should quickly respond to lawsuits, to insure that evidence explaining the facts surrounding the suit does not slip away. Too often, relevant documentary evidence quickly disappears, witnesses leave town, or memories fade. Such evidence may support the position of the defendant minister. Thus it is critical, if clergy are sued, that they immediately contact their insurance company and an attorney, so that professionals familiar with the complex process of lawsuits can advise them about what to do (and not do) regarding evidence and witnesses.

Don't Give Public Statements About the Lawsuit.

It is natural for persons who are sued to immediately want to clear themselves of any alleged wrongdoing. As noted above, this is especially true of ministers. Thus, persons who have just been sued often make public statements about the lawsuit. Ministers often make these statements before their congregations. Unfortunately, these statements often later prove damaging to their legal case. Pastors don't realize that their statements often play into the hands of their opponents. What they say (as the proverbial statement goes) is often used against them later in a court of law.

For this reason, it is best if new defendants simply say nothing until they have had a chance to speak with an attorney. It is best to respond to early questions about the lawsuit by telling inquisitive parties something like, "I'd really rather not say anything about this matter to anyone until I've spoken with an attorney." Once a defendant talks to an attorney, he or she may be advised to say something publicly that is responsive but unrevealing, such as the following:

> Serious allegations have been made against me. I strongly disagree with those who have filed suit against me. While I might like to say more, I have sought the advice of an attorney, who advises me to speak about this matter only with her. I would appreciate the prayers and

150

concerns of everyone. I have every confidence that this matter will be properly resolved in due time.

If this speech sounds like those of many high-profile political officials accused of misdeeds, that is because the very bright and expensive lawyers for those political officials told them to make those speeches. Like it or not, this is usually the best way to offer an explanation without revealing or discussing delicate facts that are better addressed in the controlled ambiance of a deposition or courtroom.

If sued, don't try to defend yourself publicly with what you believe to be clever or eloquent. Instead, be tightlipped. Seek the advice of a competent attorney.

Other than a spouse or attorney, avoid speaking with others about facts surrounding a lawsuit. After making public statements about a new lawsuit before a congregation, the next big mistake ministers often make is to call their parishioners or close friends to discuss the details of the lawsuit. Pastors often do this to ease their nerves and consciences after being accused of legal or moral wrongdoing. This is true even if they know they are innocent.

The problem with this behavior, however, is that the people with whom they speak may be called as witnesses later at a deposition or trial on the matter. If the defendant/minister has already spoken with such potential witnesses in detail about the incident, the opposing party's attorney, or the court, may determine that the person's testimony has been tainted or wrongly influenced by the defendant, thus making their testimony inadmissible. This is especially unfortunate when the tainted party would otherwise be a witness who could exonerate the minister of the charges. Again, defendants should keep their comments about lawsuits among themselves and their spouses or attorneys. Those conversations are privileged and under almost no circumstances may be required in court.

Don't decide to hire an attorney simply because the person is a member of your church. Although this is frequently done, it is a mistake. First, it may be embarrassing, or may undermine a minister's credibility to discuss delicate facts surrounding a lawsuit with a church member.

Second, it is misguided to believe that it is more spiritually discerning to hire a Christian attorney. That is no more discern-

151

ing than insisting on hiring a Christian plumber to fix your drain. I am not saying that all attorneys, like plumbers, are the same. They are not. But defendant/ministers do not need Christian attorneys; they need ethical ones who are honest and skilled at their profession, whether or not they are religious believers. There are plenty of "Christian" attorneys whose ethics and legal work do not merit that title. There are also many attorneys who claim no religious affiliation, but who maintain the highest ethical and professional standards. Hire attorneys based upon their character and skill, no matter what their religious confession.

How Clergy *Should* Respond to Lawsuits

Ministers faced with a lawsuit should do the following:

Immediately Notify Your Insurance Company in Writing.

When a person (or organization) pays an insurance premium for liability insurance, that person is essentially paying for two things: (1) coverage in the event of a finding of fault against him or her; and (2) a legal defense provided by the insurance company, in the event of a lawsuit.

This latter coverage is, in practice, often more valuable and used more frequently than the former. It means that the insurance company provides the insured person with a lawyer! This is critical, because attorneys' fees and court costs often exceed the cost of any actual liability the defendant may eventually be required to pay. Further, an insurer's duty to defend a client is broader, under the law, than the insurer's duty to pay liability costs. This means that even in cases where the insurance company is not ultimately required to pay for certain wrongful acts of an insured party, the company still may be legally required to provide a legal defense for the person.

For this reason, the first thing that ministers should do, when they or their church or organization is sued, is to notify their insurance company both in writing and by telephone. One should never presume that the claim for which he or she has been sued is not covered under the policy. Let the insurance company make such a denial. Even then, the insured person should proceed as if he or she is covered, until the insurer absolutely denies coverage in writing, or until a legal determination is made by a court of law or an administrative tribunal that the company is not required to provide for the insured party in any way. Insurance companies that wrongly refuse to provide a legal defense are frequently later required to pay their insureds enormous amounts in damage for "bad faith" claims brought by the insureds. Thus insurers rarely refuse, from the beginning of a case, to provide a legal defense.

In order for insured parties to obtain the legal defense they have paid for with their premiums, the insureds must immediately inform the insurer of any claim, and in some cases potential claim, as soon as the insured learns of it. Therefore, those who learn of a legal claim or potential claim against them, their church, or their religious organization should never delay in informing the insurance company, whether or not they agree with the claims being made against them.

Speak with an Attorney.

If a minister is sued and the insurer provides an attorney, the insurance company probably will immediately have the minister speak with that attorney about the facts surrounding the lawsuit. If the insurer does not provide an attorney, or if the minister is not covered by insurance for the legal claim, that minister should immediately contact an attorney for advice on how to respond to the lawsuit.

How does one choose an attorney? Ironically, despite the rise in the number of attorneys in the United States, it has, in many ways, become more difficult for nonlawyers to find a competent or appropriate attorney for particular legal problems. The best rule in finding a good attorney is to use the methods that attorneys use when they are sued. First, find an attorney who has some expertise in the field of law to which your legal problem relates. While attorneys sometimes advertise specialties in telephone directories or newspapers, these are not always reliable. Most of the legal problems in this book fall under the area of tort law, or personal injury defense law, also described as "insurance defense law."

A pastor should ask several attorneys he or she knows to suggest the names of those who specialize in the particular legal area for which he or she is being sued. Attorneys usually know best which other attorneys have good reputations in their field.

153

It is not unwise to find two or three with whom to have an initial consultation about the case and about fees and costs. Clients should not be embarrassed to tell attorneys openly if they are concerned about the cost, and should let them know of the limits they are able or willing to spend. Such honesty at the beginning of a case often saves everyone ill feeling later, once a final bill is tallied.

Finally, even if the price of representation is a concern, it should not be the only concern. Sometimes attorneys at certain law firms are more expensive because they are worth it. A client may spend far more for a less expensive attorney who needs to learn the substance and procedure of the law for a client's case. Conversely, an "expensive" attorney who knows the law and is experienced in litigation can often rid a client of a case more quickly and efficiently than a "cheaper" lawyer.

Handle Evidence Properly.

In addition to the warnings against speaking to potential witnesses, anyone who is sued should be cognizant of keeping papers, tape recordings, or other pieces of evidence that later may prove helpful, in the event their case goes to trial. Any such evidence should be collected and placed in safe storage. One's lawyer often is a good repository for such evidence, because attorneys have ethical obligations to safeguard it, and because the evidence is then more likely to be protected under the status of "attorney work product," which cannnot be obtained or discovered by the opposing party.

When a minister realizes that a lawsuit is imminent or is likely to arise, he or she should immediately write down or otherwise record any and all relevant facts. A court later will be more persuaded of the accuracy of facts recorded close in time to critical events, over those that a person recalls months, or even years after the fact.

In general, ministers would do well to maintain good records as a matter of course in their daily activities. Keeping accurate, adequate, and organized counseling journals, daily schedules, calendars of events and appointments, financial records, and other such documents, can save ministers from having to endure embarrassing questions or accusations later. Often these records need not be more than a brief notation to reflect a particular event or occurrence.

The Dreaded Insurance Gap

This section is not about a clothing store for hideously dressed insurance agents. It is about a potentially disastrous coverage problem that ministers (or any professionals) may face when they attempt to invoke their liability insurance for a prsonal injury lawsuit against them. To avoid this, they must pay close attention to the "fine print" of the policy.

Ordinarily, there are two kinds of liability insurance policies for personal injury lawsuits against ministers: (1) *claims-made* policies; and (2) *occurrence* policies. Typically, it is the policy (not the minister purchasing the insurance) which dictates the kind of coverage that is purchased.

Claims-made policies cover *only those claims made by a minister during the coverage period.* Thus, if a minister knows about a lawsuit against him or her, or even a potential claim, yet does nothing to notify the insurer before the policy lapses, the minister will not be covered for the claim. *Occurrence* policies *cover ministers for any occurrences within the policy period.*

Ministers should know which kind of coverage they have for two reasons. First, if they are covered under a claims-made policy, they may need to notify the insurer in writing to obtain any coverage for a given lawsuit.

Second, ministers need to avoid the "dreaded insurance gap." When a minister jumps from a claims-made policy to an occurrence policy, the minister will not be covered for work-related events during the gap period before the effective date of the new occurrence policy, and during which no claims were made under the former claims-made policy. Occasionally, ministers jump from one insurer to another because they change churches or denominations, or their churches change insurers. Whatever the reason, not being covered during this time period could lead to disastrous consequences if they are sued for an otherwise insured claim, because they would be personally liable for both their legal defense costs and any judgments determined against them in a court.

So, how can ministers be assured that they are covered for work-related events during the time period between a claims-made policy and an occurrence policy? They can purchase what is called a "tail" policy. This is simply an extended time period on their claims-made policy, under which ministers can report and be covered for any claims that arise during the gap period between the termination of their claims-made coverage and the beginning of their coverage under the new occurrence policy.

This is a fine and somewhat tedious point of insurance law, but it is one to which ministers should pay close attention, lest they experience their worst nightmare. If ministers should be sued during the gap period and have no coverage for a personal injury claim from an event that took place in the course of their ministry, they will be forced to fight not only with the complaining party, but also with their insurance company from whom they want coverage, and to whom their church has paid thousands of dollars in insurance premiums.

Read your insurance policy. Find out which kind of coverage the policy provides. Report all potential legal claims to the insurer immediately, whether you have a claims-made or an occurrence policy. When changing insurers, seriously consider asking your insurer about purchasing tail coverage for the od before coverage under the new insurance begins.

What Does It All Mean?

"[T]he whole point of Christianity is to produce the right kind of enemies."[2]   *STANLEY HAUERWAS*

What is the meaning of the flurry of lawsuits against churches and ministers in the last two to three decades? Is an increasingly godless American society actively attacking the Church? Do these lawsuits stem from an American public which views religion as a tool of the radical right and reacts by trivializing the Christian faith and treating the Church with disdain? Or are the lawsuits simply a reaction to an underregulated profession that is—in the opinion of some plaintiffs' attorneys—out of control?

I would not reject any of these suggested reasons for the increase in lawsuits against churches and clergy. However, to avoid unbridled paranoia, or an unfounded "Chicken Little theology," ministers should critique the present legal landscape in a reasoned biblical way. They should consider the following issues when asking the American legal system, Why us?

"I believe in God the Father Almighty . . . to a point"

I'll never forget a job interview I had at one of the largest law firms in the western United States. I sat down for the interview with one of the firm's chief partners.

He glanced at my resume and said, "Oh, I see you have a Masters of Divinity from Yale Divinity School. But you're not presently practicing ministry."

"That's right," I said.

He shuffled some papers on his desk nervously, then glibly volunteered, "Yeah . . . I believe in God. So tell me, do you have any other outside interests?"

The interview proceeded and ended as shallowly as it had begun. (I declined the job.)

In *The Culture of Disbelief*, Stephen Carter draws attention to the prevalence of attitudes like that of the attorney who interviewed me. Carter tells us that many in the American public, including public officials, view God as a *hobby*.[3] Popular opinion suggests that it is all right to believe in God, as long as you don't take your belief so seriously that you let it affect your life in "unusual" ways. You can tell people that you believe in God and go to church. But people become uncomfortable if you tell them that the Bible determines how you vote on issues concerning the poor, that you solicited your minister about premarital sex with a boyfriend, or that sharing your faith publicly is central to your theology.

This national condescension toward religion seems especially odd, in that the end of the century has seen a resurgence in church attendance. Despite this, innumerable ministers indicate that their churches have become filled with nonparticipating observers. This is not to say that those returning to church are not sincerely searching for spiritual meaning, or that none of them is putting their faith into action. Yet there is a demonstrable decline in consistent partipation of believers in many areas in the church, from giving to serving.[4] Such a decline makes us question the extent to which even believers have succumbed to the notion that Christianity is all right for personal devotion, but cannot meet the rigors of the streets.

The media has clearly played a role in affirming, or at least popularizing, the public condescension toward religion. From the fall of Jim Bakker in Virginia to the David Koresh incident in Waco, attentive audiences drink in dramatic media reports of religious scandals of recent decades. As with many tabloidlike contemporary news reports, media coverage of these aberrant cases often results in wild speculation and self-righteous finger wagging at the the church at large.

In light of these realities, it should not surprise Christian ministers that American society has lost its once-held reverence for them. The average minister in America is now more closely scrutinized and heavily regulated, both publicly and privately, than ever before. As for litigation against ministers, widespread media attention to the legal problems of a few clergy or religious groups has made legal challenges against all churches and clergy acceptable. Whereas suing one's minister once may have been unthinkable, it now may have become fashionable.

Too Many Lawyers—Not Enough Saints

Those who believe that American lawsuits against clergy have increased because we are an overly litigious society are, at least in part, surely correct. Lawsuits have proliferated in many fields, including medicine, law, consumer products, as well as ministry. Arguably, Christian ministers do not have a strong biblical basis for scolding society for its legal infighting. In First Corinthians 5:13, Paul directed the church at Corinth not to judge nonbelievers ("outsiders") for their bad behavior.

Can Christian communities do anything to lessen the litigation explosion, especially against churches and ministers? Despite Paul's directive not to judge secular society, Christians were told to judge the behavior of believers—"those who are inside the church." Among other things, he told Christians not to sue each other, but to resolve their legal differences outside the secular courts, through interchurch mediation or arbitaration, even if they lost some entitlements in the process (see I Cor. 6:1-7).

Because many lawsuits against clergy and churches are brought by church members who claim to be part of the Body of Christ, obedience to Paul's directives could genuinely diminish the number of lawsuits against the church and its ministers. Most denominations have elaborate disciplinary systems to address conflicts between church members, and too frequently these systems are underutilized.

Is it realistic for Christians to resolve many, if not all their disputes within the church, through arbitration and mediation? Perhaps. But these processes probably will not be adequate to address all legal violations that clergy may commit. For instance, Paul's directive that Christians not sue each other arguably does not mean that if a child of Christian parents is sexually molested by a minister, those parents should not report the crime or press charges against the minister through a state prosecutor. Although Paul directed Christians not to sue one another, he also told believers, in Romans 13:1, that they were subject to governing authorities. He certainly didn't tell his audiences that ministers who violate the law should be able to avoid the resultant criminal or civil penalties.[5]

Does Paul's prohibition against lawsuits mean that the Christian parents of a child molested by a minister should never seek money damages, to which they are entitled under civil law? Again, even though Paul discouraged believers from taking one another to court, he did not absolutely forbid such lawsuits. And as noted, he also made clear that believers were still subject to a government's penalties for illegal behavior. Christian parents who do not sue in such circumstances may send the dubious signal that they do not value the rights of sexually abused children. Arguably, Paul's language can be read to favor or disfavor pursuing these lawsuits. The determination is left to the discretion of the individual who is the injured party.

Ministers do enormous good for our society. Thus, the Christian community has strong public-policy reasons for discouraging an unlimited flood of lawsuits against churches and ministers. The emotional and financial costs of time-consuming litigation against ministers—especially lawsuits with questionable merit—will decrease the effectiveness of the valuable social service that ministers provide. Litigation against clergy increases governmental scrutiny and regulation of religion in general in America. Finally, the greatest loss to our society —as has happened to a great extent in the medical field—may be that we will squelch the desires of talented, socially minded, and otherwise willing individuals from ever even entering ministry.

A Loss of Religious Liberty? Or Wary Respect?

Many in ministry claim that lawsuits against ministers and churches are tantamount to an all-out attack on America's religious liberties. Recent court decisions such as *Oregon v. Smith* have shown an increase in the restrictions that the government is willing to place on religion.[6] However, this does not mean that the American sky is falling on our religious liberties.

When courts and legislatures act to prohibit or regulate the behavior of an individual or group, it often means that the American public has begun to view that individual or group in a new way. In many cases, it indicates that society is taking them *more* seriously, rather than less. Society recognizes that the parties it seeks to regulate have real "power" over the public.

Numerous other professionals—such as doctors, attorneys, accountants, engineers, and architects—have undergone increased governmental scrutiny and regulation as our society has entrusted them with increasing power and responsibility. The growing number of lawsuits against ministers and churches may indicate that the public believes clergy have significant influence over our society, that they are in a unique position both to help, and to harm, the American public.

A Call to Practice What We Preach

Most clergy will not view their increased subjection to lawsuits as public flattery. But no matter how clergy choose to view the increase in governmental scrutiny, one thing is certain—American society is changing its views toward clergy, religious workers, and churches.

Many believe that it is prudent public policy to monitor ministers more closely. This, it is believed, will make clergy raise their standards of care to new heights. In many respects, who can blame society for wanting clergy to improve their practices, especially after the acts of many prominent ministers during the 1980s and 1990s. Televangelists financially robbed the naive and unwary of millions of dollars under the false pretenses of helping the poor and serving the church. Pastors and priests have molested and abused the vulnerable in the most sacred and trusted circumstances—the pastor's care.

The increased governmental scrutiny of religion may, indeed, result in decreased religious liberty. But ministers should consider an alternative view of these developments. Might not the clergy also use this time of society's changing view of church leaders as an opportunity to redefine and improve the public's perception of ministry as a truly honorable profession? If, as Stanley Hauerwas says, the church is truly a "Community of Character," then should not that community's leadership be the quintessential role model of how professionals are best defined? We in ministry must accept that while the American public respects our intentions and labor, it also fears our potential for injury, if we misuse our unique positions of trust and confidence.

If there truly are issues of religious liberty to fight about in the political or legal arenas, then religious believers should fight those battles tenaciously. But it is just as conceivable that the American public simply wants its ministers to be more righteous. Society, after all, needs "saints"—exemplary leaders to follow. America's lawsuits against ministers may be viewed as a call to a higher righteousness—a higher standard of care, honesty, purity, long-suffering, and duty. If this truly is the meaning of these legal challenges, then how can we in ministry respond other than with humble acknowledgment that this was exactly our call in the first place?

Paralyzing Indecision

To lawyers, the worst kinds of judges to appear before in litigation are not those who decide against their clients, but those who simply do not decide. Instead, they try to play Solomon, cajoling the parties to cordially settle their differences.

Settling disputes can be good. But sometimes conciliation is impossible and wrong. Sometimes one of the parties is right. Sometimes parties will never decide for themselves. They need another to make a decision for them, even if it is a bad one.

At least then the dissatisfied part can appeal the case or accept the result and go on with life.

A growing number of Christian denominations have become paralyzed by indecision. The fear of legal reprisals has made it difficult for churches and ministers to make decisions and to act. We must bear in mind, however, that our present American system is comparatively supportive of the free exercise of religion. Under far more adverse circumstances, biblical figures such as Moses, Daniel, Jesus, Paul, and others are described as having acted upon their convictions, even in the face of governments that were indifferent or in oppoosition to God. Yet they acted with integrity and the power of Yahweh to continue ministry.

It is inevitable that most ministers will not be liked by all people with whom they associate. Everyone makes some enemies in life. But ministers who fail to act for fear of legal challenges become like the centipedes that lay at the side of the road because they have begun to think too much about how to walk. I pray that ministers will let their knowledge of the seven deadly lawsuits exhort them to wise, prudent, and faithful servanthood. I urge them to develop habits of integrity, but in all things, act with the conviction to which Christ has called us.

APPENDIX

---

*T*his appendix includes a brief overview of the way lawsuits work in the American legal system, a review of some of the rights, privileges, and defenses available to religious believers under the First Amendment, and a brief description of the Religious Freedom Reformation Act (RFRA).

Lawsuits in the American Legal System

1. Three Levels of Courts.

Most court systems in most states are three-tiered, comprised of a district (or trial) court, an appellate court, and a supreme court. The federal courts also are three-tiered and address questions of federal interest, such as bankruptcy, admiralty law, and lawsuits requiring the interpretation of federal statutes.

2. Filing the Lawsuit

A lawsuit is usually filed when a complaining party, the "plaintiff," files a "complaint" with a district or trial court, and then has a sheriff or constable serve a copy of the complaint and a summons upon the accused, the "defendant(s)." Plaintiffs typically must file a complaint within a certain period of time after an alleged wrongdoing, or they may be forever barred from suing the defendant because of a "statute of limitations," limiting the amount of time in which a party may sue. The time periods under statutes of limitations vary according to the state and type of lawsuit filed.

3. Responding to the Lawsuit

Once defendants are served, they customarily are required to respond formally to the complaint in the form of an "answer," within 20 to 30 days, depending on the court or state in which the suit was filed. Defendants may respond by giving one of four essential responses: (1) I admit the allegations; (2) I deny the allegations; (3) I don't know enough about the facts alleged to admit or deny them; and (4) I admit the allegations, but so what—that is, the allegations are true, but my acts were not against the law! Defendants can give these answers either in the form of an "answer" or through a variety of different motions, which ask the court to dismiss the case because the complaint is deficient in some material way.

4. Discovery and Trials

If the defendants admit the claims against them, the only remaining question may be that of the damages—that is, how much or what penalty, if any, the defendant owes because of the wrongdoing. If the defendant denies the claim in any way (which is usually the case), then the parties typically enter into a time for "discovery," wherein the parties on both sides investigate each others' evidence supporting the allegations and denials. Thereafter, the parties conduct a trial before a jury or judge (a "bench trial"), to present evidence in the form of witnesses or documents to determine who should win.

5. Out of Court Settlements and Dismissal of Lawsuits

Often, after the complaint and answer are filed, the lawsuit will end before it is fully tried, because parties settle many cases out of court. Neither party concedes that the other is correct in their claims. Instead, the parties mutually agree that certain terms are satisfactory and that they will forego the time, emotional energy, and expense of a full-blown trial, in which they may or may not be able to prove their position.

Lawsuits also are cut short when one or both parties file a motion asking the court to dismiss the case, stating that even if the facts were exactly as the other side claimed, they still would not be entitled to relief as a matter of law. Often these motions take the form of a "motion for summary judgment." Courts ultimately decide cases based upon the facts of a case, as applied to the language of a statute or a precedential holding of a previous court which dealt with similar issues. Deciding cases based upon the precedents of other courts is called the doctrine of *stare decisis*.

6. Appealing a Loss

If a case goes to trial and one party loses, or if a court summarily determines by motion that one party should be granted what they ask, the case typically may be appealed by the losing party, to at least two higher courts. Appellate courts do not usually review factual issues; rather, they review whether the lower court erred in its interpretation or application of the law to the facts, to such a degree that the lower court's decision should be reversed.

If a decision is reversed, it is often sent back down to the same lower court to be retried or for the lower court to direct a different outcome as prescribed by the appellate court. Once the highest appellate court with jurisdiction over a matter (usually the state or federal supreme court) rules on an issue, the parties are bound by that court's decision, and they may not argue the case further.

This description is highly simplified and ignores many twists and turns that the lawsuit can take. Nevertheless, it lays out the basic pattern that many court cases follow. We will explore exceptions to this pattern as need be.

Constitutional Defenses Under the First Amendment

Once religious workers and churches have been sued, their First Amendment rights are most critical, insofar as those rights may provide a defense to the lawsuit. For instance, many ministers have raised a First Amendment defense when accused of "clergy malpractice" or "breach of confidentiality," because of events that allegedly occurred in a counseling situation. First Amendment rights of religious believers are complicated, and usually are best understood on a case-by-case basis. Nevertheless, the following sketches certain key tenets of the First Amendment, as it generally applies to religious believers.

1. Neutrality Toward Religion

In the American legal system, the First Amendment to the United States Constitution provides a commitment to neutrality toward religion. The First Amendment states, "Congress shall make no law respecting an establishment of religion, or prohibiting the free exercise thereof . . . ."

Many believe that the Supreme Court has been inconsistent in applying the First Amendment to specific religious groups and individuals. However, almost all justices have historically agreed that theology and doctrine are matters of opinion, and questions of their truth should be off limits to any court or legislature. In 1871, the Court articulated this view in *Watson v. Jones:* "The law knows no heresy and is committed to the support of no dogma."

This means that no legal claim or cause of action exists, whether civil or criminal, for thinking crazy thoughts about God. Even if every other American citizen disagrees with a person's religious beliefs, that party has an unqualified legal right to be theologically wrong. Freedom of belief is absolutely protected from government interference.

2. Restricting Religious Practice

If no court or legislature may prevent or punish groups or individuals for their religious *beliefs,* what about their religious *practices?* Do people have unqualified immunity from governmental authorities, no matter how negligent or criminal their behavior, as long as they act with religious sincerity?

Clearly not. Absolute protection ends with belief. Religious believers may have the freedom to hand out literature on public streets, but they may not legally blast their message over a loud-speaker system at three o'clock in the morning in a hospital zone. Although the Supreme Court has held that certain religions may sacrifice animals as part of their religious practice, no one may lawfully sacrifice humans.

The above examples illustrate certain principles. Government may restrict religious behavior if a legislature narrowly drafts laws with the purpose of achieving a compelling government interest. Government may, in some cases, also restrict religious behavior if the interests of certain religious practitioners are outweighed by the interests of those who will suffer if their practices continue. Thus, those practicing religion in America do not have blanket immunity from government scrutiny under the First Amendment.

3. Due Process

Even if a private party or government official can leap the high hurdle of proving that someone's religious practice should be punished or cut short in some way because of competing public interests, the procedural mechanisms for punishing or stopping another party's acts are cumbersome. This is because we as Americans have another prized constitutional doctrine—*due process*. Due process is essentially the fundamental right of everyone to receive notice and an opportunity to respond when another party accuses him or her of wrongdoing. It is often said that our legal system affords every accused person a day in court through an orderly proceeding. Due process rights are intended to ensure against the deprivation of our freedoms, such as freedom of religion, guaranteed under the Constitution.

The Religious Freedom Restoration Act: Legal Renewal for Religion in America?

On November 16, 1993, President Clinton signed the Religious Freedom Restoration Act (RFRA) into law. This federal statute creates a statutory right to practice the free exercise of religion.

"But," you ask, "didn't we already have a guarantee of free exercise of religion under the United States Constitution?" Although the free exercise clause under the First Amendment of the Constitution already existed, ostensibly for the same purpose as RFRA, many have become dissatisfied—indeed, outraged—with the way the Supreme Court has interpreted the First Amendment in recent years.

In *Oregon v. Smith*, 494 U.S. 872 (1990), the Supreme Court abandoned the previously held requirement that the government show a compelling state interest before the government may impose or place a burden upon the free exercise of religion. In *Smith*, the high court found that Oregon's drug laws, which included a ban on the use of peyote, did not violate the free exercise rights of Native Americans who used peyote in their religious rites. The *Smith* decision resulted in thunderous objections from across the religious and political spectrum. From Pat Robertson's ACLJ to the ACLU, First Amendment fans stormed

Congress to change the effect of the decision. They eventually got their wish.

Many advocates for the RFRA argued that *Smith* had set a precedent for allowing the government to make greater inroads into religious liberties of all kinds. Indeed, it appeared that the high court was headed in that direction with *Smith*, when it stated, "Disadvantaging minority religious practices is an unavoidable consequence of democratic government." Such language sent chills down the spines of proponents of individual rights and caused them to proclaim that the sky was falling on our religious liberties.

However, post-*Smith* decisions by the Supreme Court regarding minority religions, made it unclear whether the court was ready to adopt completely such a narrow understanding of the free-exercise clause as was articulated in *Smith*. For example, in *Church of the Lukimi Babalu Aye, Inc. v. City of Hialeah*, 113 S.Ct. 221 (1993), the Supreme Court invalidated municipal ordinances designed to suppress the Santeria religious practice of ritualistically sacrificing animals. The *Hialeah* decision may be used to temper the effect of the Court's holding in *Smith*.

What is the greatest benefit to religious believers under RFRA? Certainty. The above decisions by the Supreme Court reveal that we live in uncertain times, when it comes to the freedom of our religious practice. The RFRA statute supposedly provides stability and, at least for now, renews our confidence that our freedom to practice our religions remains. Subsequent interpretations of RFRA by courts will tell how much certainty we have obtained.

NOTES

Consider Yourself Served:

1. The terms *ministry, minister, clergy,* and the like are used broadly throughout this book, to refer not only to ordained pastors, but also to those in any kind of religious work, including but not limited to pastors, youth workers, religious child-care workers, teachers in religious institutions, church administrators, lay ministers and counselors, missionaries in the United States, and any others who may be affected by the laws discussed in this book.

2. Historically, American law recognizes the described two types of legal violations as *malum in se* (a wrong in itself; an inherently evil and moral wrong), and *malum prohibitum* (a wrong prohibited; a wrong act simply because it is prohibited). *Black's Law Dictionary,* 5th Ed. (St. Paul: West Publishing, 1979). See Ronald Dworkin, ed., *The Philosophy of Law* (Oxford University Press, 1977).

3. Some might argue that *all* laws have a moral basis. The only distinction between law and morality is that laws are those morals about which there is such strong consensus, that those in society mutually agree to oblige one another to them. Society further agrees that if we violate those laws we will impose certain consequences on the violators, such as a fine, a prison term, or the like. Those who hold that law is fundamental to human nature, is morally based, has intrinsic value, and often believe that law has divine origins, are said to believe in "natural law." Those who believe that law is rationally based and has instrumental value, in that it serves human utility, are said to espouse "positive law." For further reading in this area, see the works of authors like H.L.A. Hart, J. H. Barns, and Ronald Dworkin.

4. This is not to say that there were not many secular influences on legal developments in the West. There were. However, the fact that much of the law as we presently know it is still traceable to Judaeo-Christian influences is important, especially in light of this book's concern with lawsuits brought against Christian ministers.

5. Tertullian, *On Modesty*, p. 77.

6. Gregory the Great, *Commentary on the Book of Job*, "Moralia in Job," xxxi, 45. Most historians would agree that the list of the seven deadly sins is much older than Gregory, dating as far back as Evagrius (364–99). Evagrius, after a successful preaching career in Constantinople, retreated to the desert monastic community of Nitria, where he became a disciple of St. Macarius. It was through Evagrius' treatise "On the Eight Evil Thoughts" that most historians presume the "seven deadly sins" found their way into Latin Christianity, chiefly through Cassian (360–435). See also M. W. Bloomfield, *The Seven Deadly Sins* (1952).

7. It has been noted that these sins are to be understood as "capital" or "root" sins rather than "deadly" or "mortal." K. E. Kirk is quoted as saying that the seven deadly sins are "sinful propensities which reveal themselves in particular sinful acts." See R. H. Mounce, "Sins, Seven Deadly" in *Evangelical Dictionary of Theology*, ed. W. Elewell (Grand Rapids: Baker Book House, 1984).

8. *Blacks Law Dictionary*, "moral turpitude."

9. *Meinhard v. Salmon*, 164 NE 545 (NY 1928).

10. M. Geyelin, "Churches, Ministers Finding Themselves Hit by More Lawsuits," *Wall Street Journal*, November 12, 1992.

11. See also J. T. O'Reilly and J. S. Strasser, "Clergy Sexual Misconduct: Confronting the Difficult Constitutional and Institutional Liability Issues," *St. Thomas Law Review* 7 (1994): 31.

1. Fraud

1. Titus 2:7-8: Show yourself in all respects a model of good works, and in your teaching show integrity, gravity, and sound speech that cannot be censured; then any opponent will be put to shame, having nothing evil to say of us.; Eph 4:1: I therefore, the prisoner in the Lord, beg you to lead a life worthy of the calling to which you have been called (NRSV).

2. This fact scenario is taken virtually verbatim from the court record in the actual case, as reported by the United States Court of Appeals for the Fourth Circuit. That record is further published at *U.S. v. Bakker*, 925 F.2d 728 (4th Cir. 1991).

3. See generally, Restatement (Second) Torts § 525 *et seq.*

4. See e.g., *Johnson v. McDonald*, 170 Okl. 117, 39 P.2d 150 (1934).

5. Usually, the *standard* for testing whether a party in a fiduciary relationship "knew" that he or she needed to tell a piece of information that he or she did not tell in order to avoid liability, is the "reasonable person" standard—i.e., a judge or jury typically will ask, what should a person of ordinary prudence, in the same circumstances as the defendant, have told? This will include the extent to which the harm done to the plaintiff was foreseeable.

6. *Heritage Village Church and Missionary Fellowship, Inc.*, 92 B.R. 1000 (D.S.C. 1988).

7. See § 101 of the Uniform Securities Act and § 17 of the Federal Securities Act of 1933.

8. 15 U.S.C. § 77x.

9. *United States v. Ballard*, 322 U.S. 78, 64 S.Ct. 882, 88 L.Ed. 1148 (1944).

2. Defamation

1. *Gorman v. Swaggart*, 524 So. 915 (La. App. 4th Cir. 1988).
2. *Hustler Magazine, et al. v. Falwell*, 485 U.S. 46, 108 S.Ct. 876 (1988).
3. This fact scenario is based on the similar, but not identical, facts in *St. Luke Evangelical Church, Inc. v. Smith*, 318 Md. 337, 568 A.2d 35 (Md. 1990). Different names were used to avoid any further embarrassment to the parties involved.
4. See generally, Restatement (Second) Torts § 558 *et seq.* In many states, plaintiffs in all cases now must prove the element of material falsity.
5. *Hustler Magazine, et al. v. Falwell*, 485 U.S. 46, 57 (1988).
6. *Gertz v. Robert Welch, Inc.*, 418 U.S. 323 (1974).
7. *Time, Inc. v. Firestone*, 424 U.S. 448 (1976); *Hutchison v. Proxmire*, 443 U.S. 111 (1979).
8. See, e.g., Utah Model Jury Instructions.
9. *Philadelphia Newspapers, Inc. v. Hepps*, 475 U.S. 767 (1986).
10. See e.g., *Hustler Magazine v. Falwell*, 485 U.S. 46 (1988).
11. See Matthew 18:15-17; I Corinthians 5; II Thessalonians 3:11-15.
12. *Joiner v. Weeks*, 383 So. 2d 101 (La. App 1980).
13. *Gorman v. Swaggart*, 524 So. 915 (La. App. 4th Cir. 1988).
14. *Church of Scientology v. Green*, 354 F. Supp. 800 (S.D.N.Y. 1973).
15. See e.g., *Stewart v. Ging*, 327 P.2d 333 (N.M. 1958).

3. Child Abuse

1. See e.g., Mo. Ann. Stat. § 556.037 (Vernon 1994).
2. See e.g., Conn. Gen. Stat. Ann. § 54-193a (West 1995).
3. See e.g., Conn. Gen. Stat. Ann. § 54-193a (West 1995); Utah Code Ann. §76-1-303(3)(1995).
4. See e.g., Mont. Code Ann. § 45-1-205(1)(b) (1993).
5. See e.g., Mich. Stat. Ann. § 767.24(2) (Callaghan 1994).
6. Public policy also encourages cases to be filed to give one who may be sued or prosecuted a sense of repose or assurance that the threat of legal action is past.
7. See e.g., Cal. Evid. Code § 1228 (West 1995); Fla. Stat. Ann. § 90.803(23) (West 1995); Ga. Code Ann. § 24-3-16 (1980); Haw. Rev. Stat. Ann. chp. 626, Rule 616; (Michie 1993); Ill. Ann. Stat. ch. 725, para. 5/115-10 (Smith-Hurd 1994); Mo. Ann. Stat. § 491.074 (Vernon 1994); Utah Code Ann. § 76-5-411 (1995); Rule 15.5 Utah Rules of Criminal Procedure.
8. "Running of limitations against action for civil damages for sexual abuse of child," 9 A.L.R. 5th 321.
9. See e.g., Wis. Stat. Ann. § 939.74(1)(c) (West 1995); Utah Code Ann. § 78-12-25.1(2) (Supp. 1994).
10. See e.g., Ill. Admin. Code, Fed. Rules of Evid., Rule 414(d)(1995); Nev. Rev. Stat. Ann. §§ 200.030 and 432B.10 (1993); Utah Code Annotated §78-12-25.1(d) (Sup. 1994).
11. Mark 10:13-16: "People were bringing little children to him in order that he might touch them; and the disciples spoke sternly to them. But when Jesus saw this, he was indignant and said to them, 'Let the little children come to me; do not stop them; for it is to such as these that the kingdom of God belongs. Truly I tell you, whoever does not receive the kingdom of God as a little child

will never enter it.' *And he took them up in his arms, laid his hands on them, and blessed them"* (NRSV; emphasis added).

12. *State v. Motherwell, et al.,* 788 P.2d 1066 (Wash. 1990).

13. Former WASH. REV. CODE § 26.44.030(1).

14. Former WASH. REV. CODE § 26.44.020(8).

15. Citing a string of United States Supreme Court cases, the appeals court further supported its ruling, noting that not all governmental burdens on religion are unconstitutional. The appellate court made its ruling even after requiring that the state show a "compelling governmental interest" to justify its regulation of religious practice—a requirement overruled in *Oregon v. Smith,* 494 U.S. 872 (1990), but reinstated under the Religious Freedom Reformation Act. (See Appendix for a discussion of these issues.)

16. For an excellent treatment generally on the variety of state child abuse reporting laws, see R. C. O'Biren and M. T. Flannery, "The Pending Gauntlet to Free Exercise: Mandating that Clergy Report Child Abuse," 25 *Loy. L.A. Law Review.* 1 (Nov. 1991).

17. ALA. CODE § 26-14-3 (1986); DEL. CODE ANN. tit. 16, §903 (1983); IDAHO CODE § 16-1619(a) (1979 & Supp. 1991); IND. CODE ANN. § 31-6-11-3 (Burns 1987 & Supp. 1990); NEB. REV. STAT. § 28-711 (1989); N.J. STAT. ANN. § 9:6-8.10 (West 1976 & Supp. 1991); N.M. STAT. ANN. § 32-1-15 (Michie 1989 & Supp. 1990); N.C. GEN. STAT. § 7A-543 (1990 & Supp. 1990); OKLA. STAT. ANN. tit. 21, § 846 (West 1983 & Supp. 1991); R.I. GEN. LAWS § 40-11-3 (1990); S.D. CODIFIED LAWS ANN. § 26-8a-4 (Supp. 1991) (any person to report only if death occurs); TENN. CODE ANN. § 37-1-403 (1984 & Supp. 1990); TEX. FAM. CODE ANN. § 34.01 (West 1896 & Supp. 1991); WYO. STAT. ANN. § 14-3-205 (Michie 1986 & Supp. 1991).

18. See e.g., ARIZ. REV. STAT. ANN. § 13-3620(A) (Supp. 1990); COLO. REV. STAT. § 19-3-304 (Supp. 1990); CONN. GEN. STAT. ANN. § 17a-101(b) (West Supp. 1991); LA. REV. STAT. ANN. § 14:403(B) (West 1986 & Supp. 1991); MISS. CODE ANN. § 43-21-353 (1981 & Supp. 1991); NEV. REV. STAT. ANN. § 432B.220 (Michie 1986 & Supp. 1990); N.D. CENT. CODE § 50-25.1-03 (1989 & Supp. 1991); UTAH CODE ANN. § 62A-4-503 (1989 & Supp. 1990); W.VA. CODE § 49-6A-2 (1986);

19. See e.g., 23 PA. CONST. STAT. ANN. § 6311a (Supp. 1991).

20. § See e.g., ARK. CODE ANN. § 12-12-507(b) (Michie 1991); CAL. PENAL CODE § 11166 (West 1982 & Supp. 1992).

21. See e.g., GA. CODE ANN. § 19-7-5(g) Harrison 1990); ILL. ANN. STAT. ch. 23, para. 2054 (Smith-Hurd 1988 & Supp. 1991); MONT. CODE ANN. § 41-3-201(4) (1990).

22 See e.g., ALA. CODE § 26-14-10; ARK. CODE ANN. § 12-12-518 (Michie Supp. 1991); KY. REV. STAT. ANN § 620.050(2) (Michie/Bobbs-Merrill 1990); N.H. REV. STAT. ANN § 169-C:32 (1990); N.D. CENT. CODE § 50-25.1-10 (1989); R.I. GEN. LAWS § 40-11-11 (1990); TEX. FAM. CODE ANN. § 34.04 (West 1986).

23. See e.g., ARIZ. REV. STAT. ANN. § 13-3620(G) (1989 & Supp. 1990).

24. See e.g., ARIZ. REV. STAT. ANN. § 13-3620(G) (1989 & Supp. 1990); NEV. REV. STAT. ANN. § 432b.220(2)(d) (Michie 1986 & Supp. 1989); UTAH CODE ANN. § 62A-4-503 (1989 & Supp. 1990); WASH. REV. CODE ANN. § 26.44.060(3) (1990). The Nevada and Utah statutes, however, recognize the minister's privilege only insofar as a person *confesses* something to the minister.

Thus, only an *offender* can confess to a wrongful act, and then later be able to assert a privilege to keep that act confidential. In the fact scenario in this chapter, it would not have done the ministers any good to live in either Nevada or Utah, because the communications were not (originally) made by the offender.

25. Again, depending on how courts interpret the United States Supreme Court's holding in *Oregon v. Smith*, 494 U.S. 872 (1990), acts by clergy like those in the Community Chapel case may *not* be considered a First Amendment violation. Cf. foot note 4, *supra*.

26. 1983 CODE c.983, § 1.

27. 18 U.S.C. § 2251 et seq.

28. See 18 U.S.C. § 2252 (a) (1,2), Supp.

29. See e.g., *U.S. v. Osborne*, 925 F. 2d 82 (4th Cir. 1991).

4. Sexual Misconduct

1. D. Dobbs, R. Keeton, and D. Owen, *Prosser, Keeton on Torts* § 930.

2. Elizabeth's lawsuit would be as successful if her husband, Dave, joined her in the suit. If both Elizabeth and Dave had gone to the minister for counseling, and Elizabeth and the minister became intimately involved, then Dave alone probably could be able to bring a successful lawsuit against the minister, under a theory such as breach contract or breach of fiduciary duty. See e.g., *Richard H. v. Larry D.*, 198 Cal. App. 3rd 591, 243 Cal. Rptr. 807 (1988).

3. See King & Woodward, "When a Pastor Turns Seducer," *Newsweek*, August 28, 1989.

4. See e.g., Minn. Stat. Ann. § 148A.01-.06 (West 1991); Wis. Stat. Ann. § 895.70 (West 1990).

5. See e.g., Minn. Stat. Ann. § 609.344(h)-(j) (West 1991); Wis. Stat. Ann. § 940.22 (West 1990).

6. See e.g., *Handley v. Richards*, 518 So.2d 682 (ALA. 1987) *(per circium)* (Maddox, J. concurring specially); *Nally v. Grace Community Church of the Valley*, 47 Cal.3d 278, 763 P.2d 948 (1988), *cert. denied*, 90 U.S. 1007, (1989); *Destefano v. Grabrian*, 763 P.2d 275 (Colo. 1988); *Baumgartner v. First Church of Christ*, 141 Ill. Supp. 3rd, 898, 400 N.E.2d 1319 1986), *cert. denied.*, 479 U.S. 915; *Hester v. Barnett*, 723 S.W.2d 544 (Mo. Ct. App. 1987); *Strock v. Pressnell*, 38 Ohio St.3d 207, 527 N.E.2d 1235 (1988); *White v. Blackburn*, 787 P.2d 1315 (Utah Ct. App. 1990).

7. One Justice of the Alabama Supreme Court indicated that clergy malpractice may be a viable remedy in that state, although that court declined to find such malpractice where plaintiff alleged intentional, not negligent, misconduct. *Handley v. Richards*, 518 So.2d 682 (ALA. 1987) *(per circium)* (Maddox, J. concurring specially). Also, a dissenting opinion in *Strock v. Pressnel*, 38 Ohio St.3d 207, 527 N.E.2d 1235 (1988) noted that malpractice is a viable action against clergy who are negligent in counseling. *Id.* at 217-21, 527 N.E. at 1244-47 (Sweeney, J., dissenting).

8. See *Lund v. Caple*, 100 Wash. 2d 793, 675 P.2d 226 (198).

9. *Destefano v. Grabrian*, 763 P.2d 275 (Colo. 1988). See also *Byrd v. Faber*, 565 N.E.2d 584 (Ohio 1991). Despite the seeming lack of success of clergy malpractice actions in negligent counseling cases, some plaintiffs' attorneys will still pursue that claim in cases involving sexual misconduct by a minister.

10. *Destefano*, 763 P.2d 275; *Erickson v. Christenson*, 99 Or. App. 104, 781 P.2d 383 (1989).

11. On November 12, 1992, the *Wall Street Journal* published an article titled "Churches, Ministers Finding Themselves Hit by More Lawsuits." Quoting from authorities knowledgeable in both law and ministry, the article explained that numerous types of lawsuits are increasingly being levied against religious workers and their organizations. In 1993, the media focused particular public attention on lawsuits against clergy and their churches or denominations for various kinds of sexual misconduct. Such news reports that the Roman Catholic Church has paid out hundreds of millions of dollars in settling such claims in the last ten years.

12. For an excellent recent article on this subject, see J. T. O'Reilly and J. S. Strasser, "Clergy Sexual Misconduct: Confronting the Difficult Constitutional and Institutional Liability Issues," 7 *St. Thomas Law Review* 31 1994.

13. Ibid., pp. 32-33.

14. Joseph B. Conder, Liability of Church or Religious Society for Sexual Misconduct of Clergy, 5 ALR 5th 530, 535 (1993).

15. *Wall Street Journal*, "Control the Damage of a False Accusation of Sexual Harassment," J. A. Lopez, January 12, 1994.

16. Ibid.

5. Clergy Malpractice

1. A fuller discussion of this topic appears in T. F. Taylor, "Clergy Malpractice: Avoiding Earthly Judgment," 5 *BYU Journal of Public Law* 119 (1991).

2. See e.g., *Nally v. Grace Community Church of the Valley*, 47 Cal 3rd. 278, 763 P.2d 948 (1988), cert. denied., 490 U.S. 1007 (1989).

3. Ibid.

4. See e.g., *Lund v. Caple*, 100 Wash.2d. 739, 675 P.2d 226 (1984).

5. For a more detailed discussion of this, see 5 *BYU Journal of Public Law* at 127-30.

6. Griffith & Young, *Pastoral Counseling and the Concept of Malpractice*, 15 BULL. M. ACAD. PSYCHIATRY L 257 (1987).

7. See, 5 *BYU Journal of Public Law* at 130-32.

8. *Nally*, 47 Cal 3rd. 278, 2980, 763 P.2d 948, 954.

9. *Nally*, 47 Cal 3rd. at 305-06, 763 P.2d at 964-65 (citations omitted) (Kaufman, J., concurring).

10. *Richard H. v. Larry D.*, 198 Cal. App. 3d 591, 243 Cal. Rptr. 807 (1988).

11. Blodget, "Religious Liability for Counseling?" 74 A.B.A. J., Aug. 1, 1986, at 30.

6. Invasion of Privacy

1. *Lewis v. Dayton Hudson Corp.*, 339 N.W.2d 857 (Mich. Ct. App. 1983); see also, 62A AM. JUR. 2d, Privacy § 48 (1990).

2. For a more general discussion of First Amendment defense, see Appendix.

3. *McNally v. Pulitzer Pub Co.*, 532 F.2d 69 (8th Cir. 1976), cert. denied 429 U.S. 855. Note that some courts add a fourth element—the absence of waiver or privilege. Id. This chapter discusses privilege under the heading "Defenses." See also, 62A AM. JR. 2d, Privacy § 91.

4. RESTATEMENT (SECOND) OF TORTS § 652E; see also, 62A Am. Jur., Privacy § 124.

5. It is noteworthy that because this false-light publication involves a minister, whose professional reputation is also likely be damaged by Pastor Harris' comments, Rev. Boyd may also have a claim for defamation.

6. See e.g., *Time, Inc. v. Hill*, 385 U.S. 374 (1967); *Hustler Magazine v. Falwell*, 485 U.S. 46 (1988).

7. RESTATEMENT (SECOND) OF TORTS, § 652A(2)(b); see also, 62A Am. Jur., Privacy §§ 68 *et seq*. See generally, *Daily Times Democrat v. Graham*, 162 So.2d 474 (Ala. 1964); *Reed v. Real Detective Pub. Co.*, 162 P.2d 133 (Ariz. 1945).

8. RESTATEMENT (SECOND) OF TORTS, § 652A; see also, 62A Am. Jur., Privacy § 251. Note: In addition to these damages, plaintiff can obtain injunctive relief or special damages in certain instances. See, 62A Am. Jr., Privacy §§ 251 and 266-67.

9. *Frio v. Superior Court*, 203 Cal. App. 3d 1480. 250 Cal. Rptr. 819 (1988).

10. *Wash. Rev. Code Ann*. § 9.73.030 (West 1988).

11. 18 U.S.C. § 2510 *et seq*. (1988).

12. *Reed v. Real Detective Pub. Co.*, 162 P.2d 133 (Arizo. 1945); see also, 62A Am. Jur., Privacy §§ 214 *et. seq.*.

13. Most states have statutes protecting the communications between clergy and parishioners or confessors. Under these statutes, a minister typically cannot be *compelled* to testify against a parishioner who has divulged private communications to the minister. This is discussed further in the chapter on Child Abuse.

14. Note: Even when the facts are known, ministers must be cautious. For example, as already noted, if an action is brought for Public Disclosure of private Facts, the argument that the facts are true is no defense.

7. Undue Influence

1. *Roberts-Douglas v. Meares*, 624 A.2d 405 (D.C. App. 1992); *O'Hearn v. O'Hearn*, 97 N.E.2d 734 (1951).

2. *Beyer v. LeFevre*, 186 U.S. 114, 22 S.Ct. 765, 46 L. Ed. 1080 (1902).

3. *In re Estate of Weir*, 475 F.2d 988 (1973).

4. In a case called *Dovydenas v. The Bible Speaks*, 869 F.2d 628 (1st Cir. 1980), such an action was brought against a minister for fraud. The judge, however, characterized the action as undue influence. The defrauded party in *Dovydenas* was a well-to-do woman, who had contributed over $6 million to the defendant church through three major gifts. The woman's family later caused her to recognize that she had been lied to and had been unduly influenced by the pastor. The pastor led her to believe that by giving the money, she would influence events such as curing illnesses or cause the release of an imprisoned Romanian minister. The Romanian minister, although real, had already been released. The woman underwent counseling and deprogramming and sued to recover her gifts to the church based upon her claims of undue influence.

As noted, the above case illustrates perhaps the most typical context for undue influence claims in ministry, namely gift giving to the church or minister. In particular, where a minister cajoles an elderly or sick person in a weakened mental and emotional state to give a large sum to the minister or church, a court may later void that gift because it was obtained inequitably, in circumstances where one person had unfair advantage over the other. The court in *Dovydenas* held in favor of the elderly woman, reasoning that she had been lied to and improperly influenced by the defendant pastor and church.

5. *Roberts-Douglas v. Meares,* 624 A.2d 405 (D.C. App. 1992).

6. *Roberts-Douglas v. Meares,* 624 A.2d 431 (D.C. App. 1993).

7. *Dovydenas v. The Bible Speaks,* 869 F.2d 628 (1st Cir. 1980).

8. See e.g., *Roberts-Douglas v. Meares,* 624 A.2d 409 (D.C. App. 1992); *First Christian Church v. McReynolds,* 241 P.2d 135 (1952).

9. *Roberts-Douglas v. Meares,* 624 A.2d 405 (D.C. App. 1992); *Nelson v. Dodge,* 68 A.2d 51 (R.I. 1949); see also *Whitmire v. Kroelinger,* 42 F.2d 699 (W.D.S.C. 1930); *Nottidge v. Prince,* 2 Giff. 246, 66 Eng. Rep. 103 (V.C. 1860).

10. *Roberts-Douglas v. Meares,* 624 A.2d 405 (D.C. App. 1992); see also *Dovydenas v. The Bible Speaks,* 869 F.2d 628 (1st Cir. 1980); *Guill v. Wolpert,* 218 N.W.2d 224 (1974); *Nelson v. Dodge,* 68 A.2d 51 (R.I. 1949).

11. *Roberts-Douglas v. Meares,* 624 A.2d 405 (D.C. App. 1992); *Molko v. Holy Spirit Ass'n for the Unification of World Christianity,* 762 P.2d 46 (1988). *cert. denied,* 490 U.S. 1084, 109 S.Ct. 2110, 104 L.Ed.2d 670 (1989).

12. See e.g., II Chronicles 31:5-6; Luke 9:62; Romans 12:1-2; Ephesians 4:11-13; Hebrews 10:25.

Responding to Lawsuits

1. From "A Letter to The Champion: a Publication of the National Assoc. of Criminal Defense Lawyers" (July 1990).

2. Stanley Hauerwas, "Preaching as Though We Had Enemies," *First Things* 53, May 1995, p. 47.

3. Stephen L. Carter, *The Culture of Disbelief* (Anchor Books, 1993), pp. 23ff.

4. See e.g., *The Abingdon Guide to Funding Ministry.*

5. Paul himself took serious action against believers who committed sins, especially those that affected others in the community. In I Corinthians 5, he demanded that the church at Corinth expel from its midst (5:13) a man who was having an affair with his stepmother (5:1). Both Roman and Hebrew law forbade such incestual relations (Deut. 27:20; Lev. 18:7-8). Under Hebrew law, this was a crime warranting the death penalty (Deut. 22:22). Paul suggests that this man's crime is worthy of death, but then indicates that there is still hope for him in Christ's salvific power (5:5).

6. 494 U.S. 872 (1990); see Appendix for a further discussion of *Smith.*